DO MONKEYS GO TO HEAVEN?

Finding God in All Creation

JOHN McCARTHY, SJ

NOVALIS

© 2014 Novalis Publishing Inc.

Cover design: Martin Gould
Layout: Audrey Wells
Cover photograph: GlobalP / iStock
Interior photos: p. 14 – iStock; pp. 33, 42, 50, 99, 120 – Jupiter Images; pp. 24, 60,
69 – Comstock; p. 79 – John McCarthy, SJ; p. 89 – Johnny Go, SJ; p. 110 – Novalis

Published by Novalis

Publishing Office
10 Lower Spadina Avenue, Suite 400
Toronto, Ontario, Canada
M5V 2Z2

Head Office
4475 Frontenac Street
Montréal, Québec, Canada
H2H 2S2

www.novalis.ca

Library and Archives Canada Cataloguing in Publication

McCarthy, John William, author
Do monkeys go to heaven? : finding God in all creation / John McCarthy, SJ.

Issued in print and electronic formats.
ISBN 978-2-89646-639-9 (pbk.).--ISBN 978-2-89646-644-3 (pdf).
-- ISBN 978-2-89646-646-7 (mobi).--ISBN 978-2-89646-645-0 (epub)

    1. Creation. 2. Nature--Religious aspects--Christianity.   3. Spiritual life.
4. McCarthy, John William. I. Title.

BT695.M33 2014   231.7'65   C2014-902664-1
                                           C2014-902665-X

Printed in Canada.

We acknowledge the financial support of the Government of Canada through the Canada
Book Fund for business development activities.

5   4   3   2   1   18   17   16   15   14

TABLE OF CONTENTS

INTRODUCTION 6

JANUARY 14
Miscarriage and the Madonna 15
In the Beginning Was the Word 16
Faith Seeking Understanding 18
Desert Solitude 20
Winterbloom 22

FEBRUARY 24
Warmth of Winter 25
Lent 26
God's Play 27
The Things We Assume 29
The Horizon of Beauty 31

MARCH 33
The Number Forty 34
Resurrection of Creation 35
O Happy Fault 36
Named into Love 38
Birdsong and Holy Week 39

APRIL 42

We Live by Touch 43

The Paschal Mystery of Spawning Salmon 44

Earth Day 45

Saltwater Crocodiles and the Beauty of Nature 47

Did Jesus Christ Save E.T.? 48

MAY 50

Body of Christ 51

Why Is the World Green? 52

This Is the Cup of My Blood 54

Love for Those Common Things 55

God on the Mountain 58

JUNE 60

Arethusa bulbosa and a Mother 61

Galaxies and God: Thumbs Up and Thumbs Down 62

Eucharist on the MV *Kouju Lily* 64

Avatar 66

Lichens and Men of the Cloth 67

JULY 69

Home Sweet Home 70

At Home in the Fog 72

Stained Glass in the Morning 74

Spirituality of Forests 75

Silence 77

AUGUST 79

Time in the Torngats 80

Labrador Journey – or What I Did on My Summer Holidays 82

Male Testes: Intelligent Design or Bad Design? 83

Saved Together 85

The Anthropocene 87

SEPTEMBER **89**

Beginnings.. 90

Moses and the Hitchhiker 92

God: A Three-letter Word 93

The Catholic Imagination.. 95

Our Genetic Heritage: In the Image of God 97

OCTOBER.. **99**

Thanksgiving..100

Let Those with Eyes See 102

Saint Kateri Tekakwitha: She Who Feels Her Way Ahead 104

Beautiful Hands of the Nail-biter Priest...........................106

Gorillas, Malaria and the Spiritual Dignity
of the Human Person 107

NOVEMBER **110**

Do Monkeys Go to Heaven? 111

Stumbling and Fumbling in the Dark................................113

Death of a Jesuit..114

Tsunamis and a Benevolent God...116

Saint Peter's Basilica and Occupy Vancouver 118

DECEMBER **120**

Advent and U2...121

Advent with Winnie-the-Pooh..122

Grace of Winter Solstice 124

Christmas Evergreen and Light...125

Passing on the Faith at Christmas 127

INTRODUCTION

W hat's a priest like you doing in the woods? Shouldn't you be in a parish, doing what priests normally do?

Such questions were common during my years of doctoral research in forest ecology at the University of British Columbia. My interlocutors were not critical in any way; in fact, they were often delighted, if not somewhat amused, to find a Jesuit priest in the forest, active in field research.

At an early age I was seduced by nature: tempted by rock, wind and water, invited by barrens, bogs and forests, infatuated by the wild, open country of my native Newfoundland. Mesmerized, obsessed, blinded, I fell for nature. The affair continues.

Nature excites my imagination. It stirs my spirit. I gravitate towards nature. I need it. Without it, I diminish. My heart, at home in nature, is stilled, focused as it is on the beauty, the plain and simple "being-ness" of natural diversity. No valuation is offered. It simply is. On a recent eight-day retreat, I spent several days in awe before the seemingly infinite crafting of form and shape offered by plant leaves. Crazy, you may think, but silence has a way of revealing what is real.

For me, nature is a path to God, pure and simple. I can explain it in no other way. By nature, I mean all that is not me, all that surrounds me, the cute and the cuddly, the wild and the vicious. As Benedict XVI stated in his encyclical *Caritas in Veritate*, nature is a "vocation" (n. 48). In other words, nature "expresses a design of love and truth" (n. 48). Nature is "wild" or mysterious, not of our making. Nature is given, a gift. Nature speaks to me of God and of God's boundless love and intimacy, and of God's unfathomable fecundity and vitality.

For some reason, nature elicits within me profound peace. Maybe that is why I spent so many years studying boreal forest ecology. Such scientific studies confirmed even more my long-held sense that science is a human quest for truth that points to the beauty and mystery of God at the heart of nature. Theological and philosophical studies have done the same for me, teasing open and revealing the wonder of the Trinity at the heart of creation.

Trinity is, by nature, relational, divine friendship. God is not One, but rather, a Community. If God is made this way, then nature must be as well. Nature is inherently of God, animated by the heartbeat of Christ through whom, in whom and for whom all things were made. Evolution speaks of the vivifying Spirit of life calling forth all into future novelty and fulfillment. And, wonder of wonders, that strange, unnerving belief that God is best known – in fact, is only known – through the Word made flesh, in the incarnational stuff of all matter.

When I entered the Jesuits in 1983 after years of study in forestry and soil science, I knew where my heart lay. Nature had to have a part. My wise novice master, Doug McCarthy, SJ, reminded me one day that I would have to make time for nature, especially in my life as a Jesuit. I would have to stay close to my source of power and energy. It was how I prayed. It was how I identified with life. It was how I found God. And probably most importantly, it was how God found me. I knew what the Scriptures meant when they spoke of a God seducing his people into the wilderness: "I will now allure her, and bring her into the wilderness, and speak tenderly to her" (Hosea 2:14).

My experience of nature has not been all honey and sweetness. Amidst my joy and exhilaration, my peace and contentment, another suite of feelings has emerged over the years. Feelings of loss and lament are never far away, it seems. I lament deeply the loss of beauty and the loss of biodiversity. In particular, I lament the retreat of natural boundaries before the seemingly relentless advance of self-made culture. The logic of development seems to know no resistance. I sense a loss of place. With the retreat of the forest or the field, it's as if I've nowhere to go. My voice falters, weakens and fades.

I've always balked at the distinction between secular and sacred. I can't live in such a divided world. I don't have the mind, or the will, for it. There exists only one world. For me, the scientific, the spiritual, the poetic, the commonsense world of the mundane are seeking the same truth by different paths. Each plays a rightful role in understanding our world. With respect to science and religion, John Paul II wrote in his June 1, 1988, letter to the director of the Vatican Observatory that "science can purify religion from error and superstition; religion can purify science from idolatry and false absolutes." He went on to note that "each can draw the other into a wider world, a world in which both can flourish."

In our current ecocrisis, we need both science and faith. Scientists need to hear from theologians, and theologians need to hear from scientists. Where once religious language and traditions were cited as the "cause" of the environmental crisis, many now realize that we fail to adequately address the ecological crisis without religious language. We also need the language of the imagination, a language that is best described as poetic, as beautiful, as hopeful.

Science, as well as technology, economics and politics, are absolutely necessary, but never sufficient. People's care for nature is based not on facts, either scientific or economic, but rather on values or principles. We care for whom and what we love. Scientific understanding will necessarily inform our decision making, but it can never decide for us what constitutes the good. Only the imaginative language of religion and wonder can do that.

The ecological crisis is not first and foremost a scientific or economic or technological crisis. It is, rather, as Saint John Paul II has noted, a "moral crisis." It speaks to our most deeply held values regarding the created world and to our sense of our place in that world. What we need, says Eastern Orthodox theologian John Zizioulas, is not an ethic per se, but rather an ethos; not a program, but a change of heart. We need religious language that speaks to the possibility of conversion or metanoia.

Only religious discourse can offer what is really needed to meet the ecological challenge. Whether we seek a new morality, a new culture, or a sense of the deeply personal and sacred order of creation, we are longing for what only religion can provide. Authentic religion invites us to contemplation before creation, to a holy vision that embraces the fullness of God's creation, to a personal and social conversion, to a dying to ourselves so that all creation may live and flourish. We seek a re-enchantment of nature as the Word and Beauty of God.

Much of what follows in my reflections flows from my years of intimacy and close contact with the natural world. My field research, my studies, my prayer, my reading, my play, have drawn me incessantly into nature.

What follows is a collection of essays inspired by my experience of nature as the theophany of the divine. I also include reflections rooted in my normal, ordinary, even mundane life. They, too, are part of the "natural" world for me.

The word "essays" seems, on reflection, to be too full a word for what follows. Musings may be more adequate – musings on nature, life, love and loss. For me, what follows speaks something of that deep, lovely, pregnant world lying beneath the veneer of the ordinary and quotidian. We call this "something" by many words: mystery, depth, meaning, spirit … maybe even love, and most certainly God.

Authentic religious faith points to this pulsing, inner, deep-down world of meaning. Call it what you will, the human heart, the soul or consciousness. Yet there exists something way deep down that defines what it means to be human. Regardless of the descriptors we may use, they all speak of that hidden depth of heart, of which the mind often knows little.

What I humbly propose is a "re-imagination" of the ordinary stuff of life. You may call it a poetry of life that attempts to point to the mystery and beauty of the divine nature of all creation.

These musings flow from my faith, my Christian Catholic faith, my love of nature, my sadness and lament at the loss of nature, my deep lifelong quest of science as a path to the beauty of God in creation. They're also my way of making sense of daily life. Many of the reflections flow from my experience of nature as salvific, from my conviction that nature is blessed with its own vocation to give honour and glory to God. You will also find much more. For me, much of life gets all mixed up – science, spirituality, God, faith, sin, hope, love, loss, wonder and tears. All we have is one world, a world so loved by God, by Mystery, that even matter becomes the way divinity is expressed. What a potentially blasphemous utterance – that the omnipotent God of infinity is known most fully in and through the flesh of the world. If that is true, and I dare say it is, then everything in every day can speak of the glory and the beauty of God.

All of creation has depth. All of nature speaks of something deep. All of life speaks volumes. Each person I meet or pass on the way has a story to tell. Each moment is unique, never to be repeated, pregnant with meaning. Yet it is we who determine that meaning, or at least catch it, make sense of it, pull it from the air. Wonder and surprise erupt and break into the dawn. Grace wings in from left field. Call it attentiveness, awareness or even innocence or naiveté. Call it what you will. There's more to life than meets the eye or the ear. Life is the unexpected. Maybe that is what Jesus meant when he uttered those provocative words: "blessed are your eyes, for they see, and your ears, for they hear" (Matthew 13:16). Or maybe it has something to do with that perennial biblical admonition: "Keep awake, therefore, for you know neither the day nor the hour" (Matthew 25:13).

You may have wondered about the origin of the title, *Do Monkeys Go to Heaven?* It's the title of one of the November reflections where I consider the fate of all creation, including monkeys, in the light of the resurrection of Christ. If Jesus Christ is truly human and truly divine, and if God's promise of life is given in the resurrection of Jesus of Nazareth, then surely this has implications for all creation, including monkeys.

I like the title. It's catchy, somewhat cheeky, and I hope provocative. Maybe it caused you to purchase the book. What I like best is that the title twins and associates what may seem like two disparate things: monkeys and heaven. We don't normally link one with the other. Yet my reading of scriptural language is that Scripture does exactly that – it associates words and things that seem worlds apart. To have life, I must die to myself. Young virgin women and old "barren" women are pregnant. The rich are sent away empty and the poor are lifted up. The Son of God is born in a lowly stable. The only crown worn by Christ the King is a crown of thorns – and on and on.

Language about God and faith is always somewhat tangen-
tial. Jesus never defines the Kingdom of God. He always professes
that the Kingdom of God is like this or like that. Hard-and-fast
definitions seem anathema in Scripture. Maybe you have felt the
same in your experience of the divine. Faith is the farthest thing
possible from clear and distinct ideas. God can never be "proved"
or "disproved" by the rational, empirical, conceptual thought
prevalent in our time. Rather, God is glimpsed, spied from a
distance, peeked at from around a corner, head and heart bowed.

As Blaise Pascal (1623–1662), the French philosopher, professed when it comes to the language and story of faith, the heart
does indeed have reasons of which the mind knows little. Jesus
would have agreed, I think. No theological discourse flowed from
his mouth, but only stories, images, metaphors and riddles. The
Kingdom of God cannot be embraced by discursive language,
but only hinted at in the lines of poetry, the melody of music, the
perspective of art and the curves of sculpture. It's a commonsense
language of weather, yeast, fishing, food and festivities.

I hope you enjoy my stories. They don't tell the whole story.
Far from it. No one person is capable of that. Rather, they reveal
what life has shown me so far. No doubt there will be more to
tell – at least I hope so. But I leave that for another day.

I suspect that you have your own stories to tell. Maybe these
readings will help to resurrect your stories of faith and wonder
and mystery. If, in reading my stories, you come to witness and
embrace the wonder and mystery of your days, I will be blessed,
and will not have recounted mine in vain.

A word on the structure of the book. The reflections are
presented in a weekly format and arranged, somewhat loosely,
according to the seasonal and liturgical rhythms of the year. You
have the editors at Novalis to blame for this. I like the arrangement and the seasonality of thought, but such was never my

intention when I began to write these vignettes. The arrangement is an afterthought. My intention was never so coherent. Rather, I wrote on whatever struck my fancy. Another feature of my attempting to see God in all things. God may have a "plan," but I must admit that my daily wanderings never seemed so purposeful.

On my priestly ordination card of 1994, you will find a quotation from the twelfth-century monk Saint Bernard of Clairvaux (1090–1153), founder of the Cistercians. In a letter to a brother Cistercian, Bernard wrote: "Believe me, you will find more lessons in the forests than in books. Trees and stones will teach you what you can never learn from masters" (*Epist.* 106). I couldn't agree more. I have learned much from the trees and the rocks and their places of solitude. May you learn even more.

John McCarthy, SJ
January 5, 2014

ACKNOWLEDGEMENTS

I need to acknowledge several people. Dr. Shirley Sullivan, Emeritus Professor of Classics at the University of British Columbia, first suggested that I write some reflections for the weekly Catholic chaplaincy bulletin at St. Mark's College–UBC. Without Shirley's request, this book would never have appeared. Joseph Sinasac, publisher of Novalis, took a chance and asked me to consider writing for Novalis. The Novalis team, with generous skill, guided the book to completion. My proofreaders, Rev. Joseph Gavin, SJ, Anne Louise Mahoney, Suzanne Nussey, Maureen Wicken, and Erica Zlomislić improved the text far beyond its primitive beginnings. Finally, I thank the Very Reverend Peter Bisson, SJ, Provincial Superior of the Jesuits in English Canada, for his generous commitment to this project.

JANUARY

Miscarriage and the Madonna

My mom suffered two miscarriages before I was born. Happily for me, she and Dad persisted. Third time lucky. For that, I am grateful.

I am reminded of this on January 1, the feast of Mary, Mother of God, and on the Memorial of Our Lady of Sorrows (September 15), when Simeon prophesied: "a sword will pierce your own soul, too" (Luke 2:35).

My mom's soul was pierced with not one, but two miscarriages, back to back. Imagine the joy of pregnancy, the expectant longing for life. She was to long for something that would never come. Instead, the birthing within would cease, and all her hopes and dreams would be dashed in a flow of blood and tissue.

I cannot imagine the pain that my mom experienced. I cannot fathom the depth of loss, the grieving, the soul searching. One miscarriage to be followed by a second. What thoughts ran through her heart when she became pregnant for the third time? She must have known that the odds were against her. Did she cry out to the Mother of Sorrows?

Maybe her prayers were answered, for on January 28, 1958, I was born, strong and healthy. As the nurse brought me to Mom's hospital bed, I wonder if Mom recalled the words of the dying Jesus as he said to his mother at the foot of the cross: "Woman, here is your son" (John 19:26). What must have moved in the heart and soul of my mom as she first held me close to her warm breast?

The Lady of Sorrows cannot simply be a Catholic thing. That the Church has promoted and developed the cult of the Sorrowful Madonna is a tribute to the rich, incarnational – indeed, universal – spirituality of Catholicism.

Who cannot relate to the weeping Mother of God? Michelangelo could only express such truth in his *Pietà*. How many women the world over, throughout the centuries, have held in their arms a loss that no one could fathom?

The Sorrowful Madonna speaks to the heart of all women, and indeed all people, who know what it means to suffer. She is universal, and by that very fact, salvific – an icon of the cradling of life's tensions of death and life.

To suffer is to live. To live is to suffer. Only the Cross will lead us to life: a truth from which we flee with every fibre of our being. If we're blessed, or just plain lucky, we will find the path that leads to life, in and through the tears of life.

I hope you don't find these words too sentimental or saccharine – or even worse, sexist and naive. All I know is that the Sorrowful Madonna speaks to a mystery to which all women and men are called. Suffering, if lived well, can create a welcoming space in our hearts. Suffering may truly gut us in a way that leaves us virginal, ready and open to receive the seed of life.

"Here am I, the servant of the Lord; let it be done to me according to your word" (Luke 1:38). Never will more courageous words be uttered by a human being. As Ron Rolheiser, OMI, has noted, these words demand a heart so pure and virginal that the only possible outcome is the birthing of God.

In the Beginning Was the Word…

Christmas is over, but I still can't get Christmas Day's Gospel out of my head. Every Christmas morning we hear the same Gospel story: the first eighteen verses of the Gospel of John.

Not fit for Hallmark Christmas cards, the words of John are strange to our ears. No mention of the baby Jesus; no mention of the stable; no mention of the shepherds in the fields or stars in the skies. Mary and Joseph and the angel Gabriel are nowhere to be found. A Hallmark nightmare.

John goes to the heart of the matter. He reaches way back into the mists of time, even to the time before time, to tell his story. And he speaks of a mystical Word. This Word in the beginning is a creative Word, for "all things came into being through him, and without him not one thing came into being" (John 1:3).

Could we not say that at the heart of creation, at the heart of nature, is the Word? There is no such thing as "pure nature." Nature is, in the eyes of faith, a "spirited" nature, animated by the Word of God.

One day, during my field research, I glimpsed this hidden Word. Part of my field work involved cutting 5-centimetre-wide discs, or "cookies," from the trunks of cut trees. During my work, I cut hundreds of "cookies" and measured the relative width of the tree rings that tell their own story of the life history of the forest.

One of those cookies now hangs on my office wall in Toronto. It comes from a balsam fir tree that was about 200 years old. As soon as I cut it from the tree in the forest, I couldn't believe my eyes. At the centre of the large cookie was this striking image of the cross. I could not have created a more exquisite image of a cross than the one that flowed throughout the wooden cookie. It was stunning.

Of course, on one level, the cross is well explained. By chance, I had made a longitudinal cut through a whorl of four branches that had broken off and had then been entombed by the diameter growth of the tree over the years.

But on another level, a deeper level for me, the cross spoke of the "Word of creation." In the heart of matter, in the heart of the beauty of nature, in the heart of the boundless diversity of life, lies a truth that speaks ever more softly. In the depth of the human soul, in the heart of creation, lies a creative and life-sustaining Word. In other words, nature has a voice, a voice that speaks of Divinity within.

The challenge for us is how to listen to this Word, how to attune ourselves to the Christic heartbeat of the world. Jesus so often proclaimed: "Blessed are your eyes, for they see, and your ears, for they hear" (Matthew 13:16). Maybe the greatest environmental gift is the listening heart, the discerning eye, the attuned ear that contemplates the heart throb of God in creation.

The Word is woven into the very fabric of life. Listen to the Word. Taste the Word. Smell the Word. Hear the Word.

"In the beginning was the Word … And the Word became flesh and lived among us" (John 1:1, 14).

Faith Seeking Understanding

I teach a graduate course entitled "Foundations of an Ecological Theology." It's a course in the theology of creation in the light of cosmogenesis and evolution. We try to engage the Catholic biblical and theological tradition in the light of Charles Darwin, the fascinating discoveries of the depth of the seemingly infinite universe, and the impact of human activity on the environment.

I don't know about the students, but I am learning a lot. They say that the best way to learn is to teach. I can attest to that. Every week I learn. I learn much in the preparation of the weekly lectures. I learn much from the assigned readings. Most of all, however, I learn from the students. I learn from their struggles, their insights, their moments of "Eureka."

Teaching and learning are flip sides of the same coin. Theology is best learned communally. I like the traditional definition of theology provided by Saint Anselm (1033–1109) in the eleventh century: *fides quaerens intellectum* – faith seeking understanding. Faith and reason are never enemies, but always friends.

I have always assumed that there is but one world. Therefore, there is nothing, absolutely nothing, that will ultimately run counter to our belief in the life, death and resurrection of Jesus Christ. Saint Paul maintained that we must assert, with gentleness and reverence, the reason for our hope (1 Peter 3:15). That hope, in the end, cannot be sidetracked or derailed by the many questions that we pose.

Push the scientific and humanistic endeavours as far as you can. Never stop questioning. Without questioning, our faith will wither and die. Questioning is central to the Catholic imagination. The insatiable desire for understanding is the heartbeat of Catholicism.

In my course, I hope to think that I present what is true to our Catholic tradition. At the same time, questions are essential. There should be no fear of heterodoxy in favour of orthodoxy. A theology class needs both.

And so, I continue to learn from the students. I am pleasantly surprised by the varied and diverse response to the weekly readings – the flash of insight, the struggle with ideas. Theology is not rocket science – it's much more difficult than that.

In the end, our finite words and ideas fail before the Mystery of God. But speak we must. We long for understanding. It's a God-given desire, that fire in the belly that drives us forth, into the depth of impenetrable mystery.

Theology is a dance, holding in tension seemingly contradictory concepts and ideas. Maybe that is the best we can do. Jesus Christ is both human *and* divine. God created heaven *and* earth. We are both body *and* soul.

And so we believe. That is our ground. But to understand … that's the difficult – and fun – part. I am grateful for the students who teach me by their questions, their struggles, their insights. I am grateful for men and women rooted in faith, seeking understanding.

Desert Solitude

During my doctoral studies in forest ecology at the University of British Columbia, one of my fellow graduate students did a most unconventional dissertation. He spent a year by himself on a small, windswept, rain-soaked island miles off the coast of southern Chile. His dissertation, entitled "A Year in Wilderness Solitude," attempted to answer this question: What are the physical, emotional, psychological and spiritual effects of living for an extended period in deep wilderness solitude? The dissertation was eventually published by New World Library in 2009 as *Solitude: Seeking Wisdom in Extremes: A Year Alone in the Patagonia Wilderness.*

I write on January 17, the memorial of another man who decided to spend time alone for an extended period – Saint Anthony of Egypt (251–356), the third- to fourth-century hermit of the Egyptian desert.

At a certain point in life, in his mid-thirties, Anthony decided to follow Christ as a hermit in the wilds of the Egyptian desert. He was venerated because of his holiness, attracted many disciples, and is considered the father of Christian monasticism.

In the Scriptures, the desert or the wilderness is presented as that privileged place of encounter with the divine. The people of Israel travelled the desert for forty years – from slavery to the Promised Land. Jesus is led by the Spirit into the wilderness, where he is tempted by the devil for forty days and forty nights.

The desert, devoid of all attraction and confusion, is a symbol of clarity and revelation. In the desert, one is forced to encounter the depths of their soul, of who they are, of what really counts.

It is not by accident that Jesus is tempted in the wilderness, which is only the desert by another name. Saint Anthony is often portrayed as one tempted terribly in the desert.

Many of us do not have the ability or even the inclination for such periods of extended solitude. But that does not mean we are not called to enter our own form of desert. We all need these desert times. Christianity calls these moments "prayer." That time of entering into the wilderness of God, when we expose our heart and soul, our body and mind, to the loving gaze of God.

Sometimes we will need extended periods of quiet and prayer to go deep within, to seek how God sees us, not how we see ourselves or how the world sees us.

Entering the world of the soul is never easy. The desert is that time of pilgrimage, of journey, when the path or destination is not necessarily clear. Enter the womb of our souls and we may be frightened by what we see. We will encounter the possibility of darkness that lies within – that same temptation experienced by Jesus, Anthony and my graduate colleague.

Our tradition tells us that unless we cross the barren desert, we will never come to really know. That's what monks tell us. Ron Rolheiser, OMI, notes that we all hold that special place within, that divine spark that will never flame out in faith, hope and love unless it is matured and quickened by the gift of the desert.

You may not get to spend years alone in the actual desert, but claim those daily desert times alone with the Trinity of Life. It will do you a world of good.

Winterbloom

I had to stop and take a second whiff. What was that? Recently, on one of my regular walks to the Spanish Banks in Vancouver, I was sideswiped by an amazing, sweet, spicy aroma. Nothing like Chanel No. 5 or the latest Parisian scent to turn the head or the heart. But this scent emanated from a gorgeous, yellow-floraled shrub called the witch hazel or *Hamamelis mollis*.

The colourful shrub also goes by the name of Winterbloom – appropriate, given its ability to bloom during the winter. A true harbinger of spring, even if the beginning of spring is officially weeks away.

According to the ancient writer of Genesis, on the third day, the earth brought forth vegetation, plants yielding seed of every kind, and trees of every kind bearing fruit with the seed in it (Genesis 1:11-12). Nice to read that the earth "brought forth" the world of plants. They were not created from on high, but were enticed to spring forth from the womb of the earth.

Forty days after the winter solstice (a nice biblical number), you can see signs of this springing forth. The Winterbloom is exemplary, but other signs are beginning, too. Buds are swelling in the forest; red alder catkins have appeared.

Each spring in the northern hemisphere, the earth brings forth a symphony of colour, form and sight. Days lengthen, the sun's warmth increases, ice melts, migrants move, sap flows, buds burst and lovers find solace in each other. The seasonality of life repeats itself with assuring regularity. Out of the dead of the earth gushes life. Time to migrate. Time to build nests. Time to flower. Time to tap the sugar maple. Time to plan for the summer nuptials.

Earth is generative. Jesus said he came so that we may have life and life to the full (John 10:10). In him and through him and for him all things were made (Colossians 1:16). Jesus Christ is the cosmic tree, rooted in the stuff of the earth, reaching up to the boundless heavens. The sap of the Spirit never fails to rise up through the Body of Christ. Somehow, Christ is Love hidden deep down within. And from deep within, the Tree of Life bursts forth the spring of life: buds pulsing, sap cruising, roots gripping, lovers caressing.

Jesus Christ won't let go of this world, for Christ is at the heart of this world. As the earth flushes forth in hope each year, so do our hearts yearn for life, for goodness, beauty and truth. These are the waters of life welling up within us, springing forth from the Spirit within.

And so amidst the shedding of winter signals the Winterbloom – a precursor of things to come.

FEBRUARY

Warmth of Winter

G rowing up in St. John's, Newfoundland, I would love it when a hefty snowstorm would shut down the city. For days, the strong northeasterlies blew in off the North Atlantic. The seemingly relentless snow-laden howls whistled the wires, whitened the landscape and scurried through every drafty nook and cranny in our house.

If we were lucky, we would lose power. Somewhere down the line, in the back hinterland, some section of the towering hydro lines would succumb to the burden of snow, rime ice and wind. Down it would bend, honouring the power of the winds.

The impending darkness and cold brought forth our candles and huddled our family together in the living room. I delighted in those times. The laughter and coziness amidst the flickering flames still warm my memory.

Out would come Dad's Coleman stove, that trusty companion on many a trip into the woods – and now our saviour in the chilled house. At night, Mom would tuck us in extra tight under the heavy coloured quilts, leaving only our noses to welcome a pinch of cold.

Our morning eyes opened to a bedroom icy still. We dared not move our warm toes too far afield. Our gaze rested on the frost-gilded bedroom window. Tracing my warm finger over the icy fans and feathers, I etched translucent trails upon the wintered pane.

After the storm had passed, with abandonment and excitement, we burst forth from our frosty hovels to find a city hushed beyond belief.

The normal confines of the city had been obliterated by snow and wind. Where once roads provided passage, snow dunes now signaled new routes for all of us energetic young children. Tops of telephone poles had grown closer. Cars had disappeared.

What wonders those northeasterlies had created, piling up snow in shape and form never imagined. The wind-hardened curves and crests created a dream world to our young eyes. New lands to explore, snow caves and tunnels to create, mountains to ascend and claim.

And the silence. Oh, what blessed silence had befallen the city of enterprise. Hushed – no planes in the sky, cars frozen silent, bent humans here and there, shovel in hand, carving a way through the mounds of snow.

I currently live in balmy Vancouver. I am fine with the rain and mist because I have neighbouring mountains covered in snow. The best of both worlds, one could say. At least you don't have to shovel the rain, many a Vancouverite will profess. At the same time, I sometimes hanker for a hell of a good snow – the kind that shuts down a city, huddles people together and unleashes a child's imagination.

Lent

The joyful season of Lent approaches – a time of preparation for the great joy of Easter.

Ron Rolheiser, OMI, says that we can celebrate only after we have prostrated ourselves in ashes. We can quench our thirst only when we have crossed the dry and parched deserts. We can feast only after the purification of fasting.

I never used to pay much attention to Lent. I used to look forward to Pancake Tuesday, though. Greatly anticipated were the nickels and dimes hidden in the pancakes dished up by Mom. Then there was the Lenten Folder. Each day I would carefully slip a newfound quarter into the cardboard slot, vaguely aware that the money would be put to good use somewhere.

As I got older, Lent assumed greater meaning. Call it wisdom – or just plain mundane experience – but I now need Lent. I need that time to ponder, to wait, to sit in ashes, if necessary, and to let God do what God does best – mould and fashion me, and at times break me to start over again.

I have come to see the value of fasting. Going without focuses the Lenten period of forty days.

That time-honoured period of forty – Israel wandering in the desert for forty years, forty days and forty nights of the Flood, forty days of Jesus tempted in the desert. We need time to die to ourselves and so live for the world.

Lent provides that time. Let us enter it with joy and hope.

God's Play

I don't get time to play with children very much.

There's an obvious reason for this, given that I am childless. So, I tend to deal with so-called adult things. Now, you may be thinking of such things as "adult entertainment." While such may have its own seductions, I am thinking of more mundane things, such as meetings, preaching, and paying bills. That's why it was so nice recently to play with children of good friends of mine. I am thinking in particular of two young girls, daughters of two different families.

The father of one of the girls wrote me after my day-long visit: "My daughter got you to read books to her, to take her out in nature, look at her drawings, watch her jump over a Tim Horton's cup, play a board game, take pictures which now turn out to be a video, share meals, and then a hug goodbye."

With the daughter of another friend, we got to toboggan down "Rocket Run," prepare the raspberry and agave topping for the dessert, watch her favourite *Max and Ruby* cartoon, and build towers and castles.

Play is essential to the spiritual life. Maybe that's why Jesus encouraged his followers to become like little children. He even suggested that unless you become like little children, you will never enter the Kingdom of God (Matthew 18:3). Strange, tough words.

Obviously, Jesus is not calling us to forget our mortgage or forgo our favourite Scotch. We are no longer children. But there is something of the child that we must hold on to – and that is the universal call to play.

Watch a playground full of squealing and laughing children. Hair flying, gleeful cries of delight, abandoning themselves to the moment. No past to haunt them, no future to worry them. That will come, but for now they delight in the moment, for that is all there is.

How to guard that truth of the moment, or that "naked now," as some spiritual writers describe it?

Collecting lichens does that for me. Wherever I travel, I focus on the diversity of lichen life that surrounds me. The lichens focus my attention and fill it with delight. Maybe that is a good definition of play – focused delight. Not a bad descriptor of prayer as well. Climbing Vancouver's Grouse Mountain and hiking or snowshoeing in the backcountry – that does it for me as well.

Playing with my friends' children drew me into worlds that I had somehow forgotten. From one perspective, the world may be going to hell in a handbasket, but here we were reading of the magic and wonder of Snow White or succumbing to gravity down Rocket Run. Each page opened a world of wonder. Each run down the snowy hill drew us into the depth of God.

Play cannot be left only to children. They come by it naturally. We adults, however, have to make time for it, carve out a space for it. Otherwise, we become old and hardened before our years. Or, we may trip up in the many forms of "adult entertainment" that seduce us into sadness.

Become, therefore, like little children – and enter the Kingdom of God.

The Things We Assume

How often have you heard that the Catholic Church (or Christianity in general) is the cause of our environmental woes or a hindrance to scientific advancement? I have often come across such ideas.

Such notions, of course, are pure poppycock.

I stumbled across two interesting stories today about two Catholic priests: one an environmentalist, the other an astrophysicist. Both are diocesan priests (all can't be Jesuits, of course) – one is from the Philippines, still alive; the other is a Belgian who died in 1966.

The $150,000 Goldman Environmental Prize is the world's largest prize honouring grassroots environmentalists. Six winners are announced each year. The winner of the 2012 Islands and Island Nations Goldman Environmental Prize was Father Edwin Gariguez of the Philippines.

For years, he has been battling the Philippine government and the Norwegian mining company Intex, which launched open-pit mining of nickel on the island of Mindoro in the late 1990s. If you read the mining company's website, you would think that the mine was the best thing since sliced bread. Father Edwin and many others thought differently. As a result of their efforts, the Philippine government halted the mine in 2009. The saga continues.

My second priestly encounter was an article in a recent issue of *Nature*, the prestigious British science magazine. The story concerned who should be given credit for one of the most profound discoveries of our time: that the Universe has a story, that it is expanding, and that it therefore had a beginning.

You have probably heard of Edwin Hubble, the American astronomer after whom the Hubble telescope is named. In the English-speaking world, and particularly on this side of the Atlantic, Hubble is credited with the idea of an expanding universe.

But it was in fact a Belgian priest, Monsignor Georges-Henri Lemaître (1894–1966), who proposed the novel idea that the universe was expanding. His only fault was that he published his brilliant idea in French, in a relatively obscure Belgian journal, *Annales de la Société scientifique de Bruxelles*. Lemaître's original ideas appeared in 1927. Hubble independently pronounced the same idea of an expanding universe in 1929. It wasn't until 1931 that Lemaître's 1927 paper was translated into English and published in the *Monthly Notices of the Royal Astronomical Society*. You see the problem.

To make matters even worse, Lemaître himself deleted from the 1931 translation his description of what later came to be known as Hubble's law. Why? Given that Hubble's account had been published in 1929, Lemaître apparently saw no need to repeat in the 1931 translation his more tentative findings from

1927. This proves that the early bird doesn't always get the worm. But the next time someone claims Hubble as the discoverer of the expanding universe, kindly refer them to Lemaître's 1927 paper. There is little doubt that Lemaître deserves the credit.

By sharing these two stories, I in no way wish to indulge in gleeful Catholic apologetic handwringing. I wish to simply note that things are not always what they seem. Sometimes we have to move beyond the stereotypes or our gladly held assumptions. That's a good lesson for us all.

The Horizon of Beauty

It's beautiful from where I write here at Loyola University Chicago, the Jesuit university on the shores of Lake Michigan. The early dawn light catches the waves in motion, whitened caps the only indication of the energy of wind, water and wave.

The waters of Lake Michigan stretch to the warm horizon. I love horizons. They embrace me somehow. My heart and mind want to expand to meet the infinity of distance. Growing up on the shores of the North Atlantic must have done that to me. And so, on the shores of Lake Michigan, it's good to be here. To simply rest and gaze into the distance – nothing more I want at this moment.

Beauty has that effect on us – we simply wish to rest before it. Beauty attracts us, lures us, seduces us. Beauty calls us into rest.

Beauty has many forms – physical beauty with that alluring symmetry of form and movement, the beauty of nature, the beauty of truth, the beauty of goodness and wisdom.

People often ask me why I study lichens. Sophisticated answers never seem to satisfy me. I study lichens, just as I studied forests, simply because I find them so beautiful. Now, when someone queries me about the source of my attraction to lichens,

I simply say that lichens are lovely. No other reason suffices. I think that's why most scientists study what they do. They simply are attracted by the beauty of beetles, stars and gazelles.

Over the past several months, I've travelled far and wide – from Nairobi to Munich to Helsinki, on to Vancouver, Managua and Chicago – and much more in between. I've witnessed much beauty, as well as its absence. It seems that the absence of beauty is just as striking as its presence.

The challenge for me is to see beauty (or God) in all things. For does not Scripture remind us that nothing can come between us and the love of God (Romans 8:38-39)? Even the darkest pit of hell could not escape the resurrected beauty of God.

At the same time, the absence of beauty invites, if not demands, our response. It's easy to rail against the darkness – and that we must, at times. But a more difficult task awaits us. And that is the task that creates beauty.

God is Beauty. Because of that we are made for beauty, we long for beauty, we are most human when we build beauty.

Blessed Mother Teresa spoke the famous words about doing something beautiful for God.

So go ahead. Speak a kind word, write a poem, protect a forest, lend a helping hand, guide a child to grow strong and free in faith, make love, cultivate flowers, draft fair and just laws, welcome the weary and weak. It's only because of what you do that the world will be a better and more beautiful place.

Do something beautiful. By its very nature it will necessarily be of God.

MARCH

The Number Forty

Forty is a special number in Scripture.

During the Flood it rained for forty days and forty nights. The people of Israel wandered for forty years in the desert seeking the Promised Land. Moses spent forty days and forty nights on the mountain before he received the Ten Commandments. Before he goes public, Jesus spends forty days and forty nights in the desert.

Because before Jesus goes public, he needs to enter into the depths of his soul. He has to enter the darkness of his own temptation. Note that Jesus was led into the desert by the Spirit. Without this, Jesus could not continue.

Lent has always been understood as a time to imitate this action. As Ron Rolheiser, OMI, reminds us, Lent invites us to metaphorically spend forty days in the desert like Jesus, to face our own demons and to wait for the angels of the Lord. It's painful, sometimes bloody, but without engaging the desert of our lives, we fail to rejoice in the blessed oasis of redemption.

Enter Lent as fully as you can. Resist your dilly-dallying. Let your soul be deepened by prayer, fasting and goodness. Only then will the angels of the Lord come to save you. Only then will you be set free to love: to love God, to love the world, to love yourself.

Resurrection of Creation

The celebration of Easter changes with the cosmos. Easter is a "moveable" feast. Unlike Christmas, Easter is celebrated on a different date each year. We celebrate it on the first Sunday after the first full moon of the spring equinox.

In the northern hemisphere, Easter signals the time of rebirth, the strengthening of the sun, the fresh beginnings of the new life of spring.

It's no wonder that the Church decided to fix Easter to the timing of spring. Easter is a celebration of life. Earth flows with the sap of life, budding leaves and flowers, sugared sap cruising the innards of trees, pulsing forth life.

The sun returns to the northern hemisphere, erasing the snows of winter to reveal a browned earth eager to green and ripen under the freshening rains and solar warmth.

If one can claim a heart to Christianity, it would be its drive toward life. God is revealed as the creator of life. Jesus Christ is the way, the truth and the life. The Holy Spirit is the giver of life. We are called to life in the Spirit.

The Easter Triduum celebrates the deepest mystery of creation – that at the heart of creation, of all reality, is the pulsing beat of life. A brutal instrument of death is transformed into the tree of life. Jesus Christ, lifted up on the cross, becomes the sign of life for all creation. Conversion is possible. Death has lost its sting.

On Easter Sunday, we not only celebrate the resurrection of Jesus Christ; we also celebrate the resurrection of creation. Resurrection of the God-Man prefigures the resurrection of creation. According to Karl Rahner, SJ (1901–1984), the resurrection of Christ is the beginning of the divinizing transformation of all things – the beginning of the ontological transformation of the entire creation.

Because of Easter, the heart of all matter is "resurrectional." In other words, at the heart of creation is this relentless urging towards life. Deep within matter lies this hidden spark of life, resurrected life. Matter has self-transcended into life, life into conscious life, conscious life into human life, human life into Christic life.

Christ is the radical self-transcendence of the created universe into God. In the Paschal Mystery of Easter, evolutionary history gives itself into God and is taken up and transformed in God, as the beginning of the reconciliation and transformation of all things in God.

At Easter we proclaim that Jesus Christ is risen. In the same breath we proclaim that all of creation is risen as well. Death is not the final word of the world. Death is not the final word of our lives. A new heaven and a new earth await.

Life is the thrust of creation. Resurrection is the fullest meaning of creation. Today we celebrate life and resurrection. Christ is risen: Alleluia, Alleluia!

O Happy Fault

Are you weak enough to be a follower of Christ?

I've been struggling with this question for some time now. Maybe it's got something to do with Lent. Or maybe it's got more to do with that time of my life when I am past any illusion of personal grandeur or salvation through right works. I know only too well the furious weakness that often assails me.

The primal myth for understanding human weakness and temptation surely has to be the Fall. It all sounds so final and clear-cut. Adam and Eve, the primordial couple, each gave into temptation. Their eyes were opened, they saw their nakedness, and they hid from God in shame. From the Garden they were expelled, each with their own curse to bear.

The Fall has always been interpreted in somewhat negative terms. We fell, therefore we needed a saviour to bring us back. In the Easter Exsultet, do we not proclaim, "O happy fault of Adam which has gained for us so great a redeemer"? I get that and buy into it – at least partly.

But what if we turned our reasoning upside down? What if we professed that the Fall of our primordial parents was something that had to happen? What if we sang at Easter, "O happy fault of Adam, without which we could never have become human"? What do you think of that?

Can we ever think of the Fall as a "good" thing? Such thinking seems downright dangerous, if not unthinkable and unutterable, indeed heretical. How could such sin, shame and expulsion be good? Or if "good" is too strong a term, how about the "necessary" fault of Adam? But, regardless of whether we consider the Fall good, evil or even necessary, the fact is that it happened.

And because it happened, our eyes were opened. For me, that is the key insight in the story of the Fall. It seems to imply that without the Fall, our eyes would have remained closed; we would have stayed in the Garden. But in fact, our eyes were indeed opened; we left the Garden (albeit this was God's decision, not ours), so we would have to begin our journey and find our way. It's as if we had to leave the Garden to grow up as humans. Maybe it's like leaving home. We all have to leave the safety of home to grow up. Maybe that is why the Fall may be considered "necessary."

Richard Rohr, OFM, in his book entitled *Falling Upward: A Spirituality for the Two Halves of Life*, says the following: "Losing, failing, falling, sin, and the suffering that comes from those experiences – all of this is a necessary and even good part of the human journey." The title of his book tells it all. To advance and grow in the spiritual life, the only way "up" is "down."

Remember the words of Jesus: "Very truly, I tell you, unless a grain of wheat falls into the earth and dies, it remains just a single grain; but if it dies, it bears much fruit" (John 12:24). Or the haunting admission of Saint Paul: "... for whenever I am weak, then I am strong" (2 Corinthians 12:10). The resurrection of Easter is possible only after the death and annihilation of Good Friday.

I wish it could be different. I wish I could grow spiritually without having to suffer. However, I know it can never be different. Our eyes have been opened. We have been thrust from the safety of the Garden into the hazardous and dusty journey of life.

For some reason, the only way "up" is indeed "down." May God not stray too far from us on our way.

Named into Love

One of my favourite lines in scripture is John 20:16: "Jesus said to her, 'Mary!'"

With one word, the resurrected Christ transformed the life of Mary Magdalene.

Mary stands weeping outside the empty tomb. The love of her life had just been ripped away. He is nowhere to be found. The tomb is empty. But Love's desire is never quenched, even by the separation of death.

She saw a man, but he was simply the gardener. She was blind to the wonder that stood before her. But once Mary heard her name, her life would never be the same. One word: that's all it took.

How she must have longed to cling to her beloved. Instead, Jesus transforms her into the first apostle. Go, he says, and announce to the world what you have seen.

Express the name of another in love and witness their transformation. Watch their heart and mind expand and fill with delight. Witness their energy for good. Watch them transform into holiness.

What power we hold on our tongues. The power of life – or the power of death. Even Scripture says that the most powerful weapon is our tongue. It can give life. It can snatch away life.

Think of the last time your name was spoken in love. What stirred and moved within you? There may be no greater gift than we can bestow on another than their name expressed in love.

You shall not take the Lord's name in vain. We know this as one of the Ten Commandments. No less important is the commandment not to take each other's name in vain. A person's name – what a unique and special mark of that person.

So, my friends, take care with people's names. How you utter the name of another is a matter of life or death. Mary Magdalene recognized her Beloved after she heard her name spoken in love. May you instill that same life in others.

Birdsong and Holy Week

"Lord, help me to get through this day."

From the slumber of sleep, these words greeted my day. Yesterday was full from morning till night. No respite in sight again today – or for the rest of Holy Week.

Holy Week – I had better words for this week that seemed to pull no punches, take no prisoners, or give any rest to the weary.

That morning, I knew I had to commit to my prayer before anything else. If I left it until later, it would never happen. Sure, there was important work to do – deadlines to meet, phone calls and e-mails to answer, not to mention the many details of the fast-approaching Easter Triduum. Some people would ever call it God's work (*Opus Dei*) – but I knew that without my morning prayer, the work would not be of God.

While at prayer, I am blessed to look out through my rather large window onto a leafy backyard and laneway. Close to my window, an old lilac and an apple tree break the monotony of the evergreen cedars.

In the blink of an eye, they swept in to settle in the sunlit early spring branches of the lilac tree. Within a flash, the lilac was transformed. The avian flash mob had descended, turning the early morning radiance into a melody of dawn chorus.

For some, such birdsong, or, if you prefer, avian vocalization, is simply the result of evolutionary pressures that enable birds to describe and maintain territory, to reproduce well and to spread those "selfish genes." That may be true, but that is like stating that fine Scotch or wine is simply the product of anaerobic ethanol fermentation of sugars. They are that indeed, but the "gladdening of men's (and women's) hearts" (Psalm 104:15) is how the Bible likes to describe such distillation and fermentation products. The same goes for the heart-warming melodies of the spring passerine birds in the lilac tree in my backyard.

Regardless of my epistemological perspective that early morning, the sweet song of the dawn did much to raise my prayer to heaven. In fact, I dare to say that the birdsong *was* my prayer to heaven.

My eyes blinked open that morning with much on my mind. The coming day seemed too short to possibly embrace all that awaited me. During such times, my mind is prone to anxiety. How in heaven's name will I get through all this?

But along comes a chorus of song from out of the blue – literally. It awakened other thoughts – the beauty of God's gift of creation, the pure gift of that unique moment unknown to any other.

I felt it as a call to simply trust the day, to let it gently unfold. I rested easily into prayer. I gave over the moment to God, to mystery, to my inability to control life.

That's a form of resurrection. It may not sound like much. It won't make the Catholic headlines or compete with the Shroud of Turin. But resurrection is new life, transformed life, glorious life in the Spirit – no matter how it happens. It is never a one-shot deal, never simply a resuscitation, but a transformation into something unknown and brand new.

That morning the impossible happened. Resurrection is like that.

APRIL

We Live by Touch

W e live by touch. Touch is essential to early infant development. Sexual relationships are a privileged and sacred form of touch. The resurrected Jesus Christ invites Thomas to touch his wounds.

Human touch comes in many different forms. The touch that heals, the touch that grasps and covets, the touch that calms and reassures. There's the touch of love, the touch of hate, the touch of sexual intimacy that forgives and unites, the touch of rape, incest and pedophilia.

Jesus is described as the one who touches. He touches the untouchables, the sick, the lame, the lepers, the destitute, the demonic, the deaf and the forlorn. The touch of Jesus heals and forgives.

We hear much these days of the wound that afflicts the Body of Christ – the wound of pedophilia. The Church has no monopoly on this wound; the data show otherwise. But, regardless, the wound still festers and pains.

All of us have our wounds. The Church, the Body of Christ, has its wounds. Maybe that is why the resurrected and glorious Christ is the wounded Christ. One would have thought that if God could raise Jesus from the dead, he would certainly have bandaged up those awful wounds. But no, the wounds remain. For us, they are glorious wounds. They remind us that we are in constant need of healing. The Church is in constant need of healing. That fact should help us to love the wounded Church, our wounded humanity and our wounded Earth.

Jesus Christ invited Thomas to touch the divine wounds. We, too, are called to that same act of love. For only by touching the wounds of the Body of Christ will we come to believe.

The Paschal Mystery of Spawning Salmon

We circled the helicopter several times to let the grizzly and black bears know we were dropping by. Bald eagles emerged from the old-growth cedars to drift away from our approach. Into the river valley we descended. The fall-yellowed alder leaves scattered wildly and the approaching river misted our windows. Ever so gently, the pilot positioned the chopper onto the rocky shores, feeling out a safe and level landing spot. The earth tested, the chopper eased onto the riverbank.

The stench of rotting flesh flushed our nostrils as we opened the doors. Spawning salmon limped away from our approach. Large red, rotting salmon lay spent along the sandy banks. Fresh bear tracks marked the sands. Red salmon flesh, exposed by the foraging bears, brightened the otherwise drab wet sands.

As we walked the fleshy, putrid shores, the Coho salmon flapped and swam their last moments. Bleached salmon bodies draped rocks and logs like limp carpets. Empty sockets, hooked jaws, protruding teeth, gaunt faces marked our every gaze. They had done their duty, returning to ancestral streams after years in the Pacific Ocean. The future was now assured.

These "salmon forests" have witnessed this annual self-giving for generations – this dying so that others would live. The future was established, not only for the salmon, but for the bears and eagles – and the forests that scavenged this feast of flesh.

This cycle of death and dying is known by all creatures, including us. We may fear it, resist it, not have much sense of it, but that doesn't matter. It's commonplace and relentless. It's built into the very fabric of all life on the planet.

It's as if the dying and resurrection of the Christ event is the hidden truth of all creation. The dying and rising of Jesus Christ was not simply an historic event that marked the foundation of Christianity. It was that, but it is never a moment in the sense of past and finished. It's enduring, never-ending. In a word, it's eternal. It's of God.

And because it's of God, the Paschal Mystery speaks of universal, timeless truth – a truth that links heaven and earth, life and death, light and darkness, hope and despair. As the salmon die only to make way for the future, we, too, are called to die each and every day so that the world may live.

Die to yourself, Jesus tells us. Let the first be last and the last be first (Matthew 20:16). The Paschal Mystery transcends all matter to enter the heart of the spirit.

As we prepared to leave this river of life, the spawning salmon, red in anticipation, scurried away in the swift-moving, shallow waters. We left them to continue their age-old ritual of death and rising. We have given it a name that is above all other names – the death and rising of Christ Jesus. This Mystery knows no bounds. It moves the salmon as it moves our lives. Nothing is unaffected by this ancient, abiding mystery that calls all creation to new life. I have come that you may have life and life to the full, promised our saviour Jesus Christ (John 10:10). New life for all, for the spawning salmon, for you and me, indeed, for all creation.

Earth Day

April 22 is Earth Day. The first Earth Day was celebrated in the United States in 1970. In 1979, Pope John Paul II declared Saint Francis of Assisi as the patron saint of ecology. The first papal statement dedicated to ecological issues was John Paul II's

1990 World Day of Peace message. It was appropriately entitled "Peace with God the Creator, Peace with All of Creation." Twenty years later, in 2010, Pope Benedict XVI issued a similar World Day of Peace message entitled "If You Want to Cultivate Peace, Protect Creation."

A particular strain of Christian thought assumes that the real drama of any consequence is between God and humanity. Nature is seen as being of little consequence from a religious or theological perspective. In fact, nature is often considered as simply the stage upon which the all-important drama of human salvation is enacted.

Three things have radically changed this perspective. First is our knowledge of humanity and all of nature as a function of what we may call deep space and deep time. The universe has a story. Humanity has a story. For the universe, it's the 13.8-billon-year-old story of the expanding and developing universe since the so-called Big Bang. For humanity, it is the amazing story of biological evolution and a common ancestry with all of life.

Second is the *Apollo* spacecraft photo of our home planet Earth as a marvellous, fragile blue-and-white orb hanging over the scarred and cratered surface of the moon at close quarters. That photo changed humanity's view of itself forever and is said to have launched a thousand environmental movements.

Third is the sobering realization that we live on a human-dominated planet. Our activities have far-reaching effects, from changes in the Earth's climate to the engineering of life itself. Our impact is ubiquitous.

This threefold experience is novel. Past human generations never understood themselves in these ways. We are challenged to rethink our role in the great scheme of things. Let us turn to our rich theological and spiritual tradition for help.

Saltwater Crocodiles and the Beauty of Nature

"Who is not enlightened by such great splendor in created things is blind; whoever remains unheedful of such great outcries is deaf; whoever does not praise God in all these effects is dumb; whoever does not turn to God after so many sighs is a fool. Open your eyes, therefore; alert the ears of your spirit, unlock your lips, and apply your heart that you may see, hear, praise, love and adore, magnify, and honour your God in every creature" (Saint Bonaventure, *The Journey of the Mind into God,* 1:15).

On April 28, 2010, Lauren Falls, a twenty-five-year-old New Jersey university student, was killed by the largest of all living reptiles. On that day, while swimming off the Andaman Islands on the east coast of India, Lauren was attacked by a saltwater crocodile and killed.

I never knew that such beasts existed. Saltwater crocodiles (*Crocodylus porosus*) are large beasts – and apex predators. Weighing in at over one tonne and up to 5.5 metres in length, the saltwater crocodile knows no enemies. They command the waters off northern Australia, eastern India and Southeast Asia.

I recently read Jame Schaefer's book *Theological Foundations for Environmental Ethics: Reconstructing Patristic and Medieval Concepts* (Georgetown University Press, 2009). Chapter 3 is entitled "Appreciating the Beauty of Creation." Schaefer recovers theological notions of the beauty of creation from early Patristic and Medieval sources.

I am quick to wax poetic, somewhat eloquently, when it comes to the beauty of nature. However, when I think of the saltwater crocodile, or the inland taipan of Australia (400 times more poisonous than your run-of-the-mill rattlesnake), or the AIDS or Ebola virus, I am tempted to refrain from my celebration of the beauty of nature. Things get too close to home and I get the jitters. Where are Bambi and Peter Rabbit when you need them?

I remember once standing on some rocky crags overlooking a raging North Atlantic off the coast of Newfoundland. I love going to the coast in a storm. On that day, though, as I gazed into the restless swells and whitecaps of the wintered North Atlantic, I was overcome by fear. That seething ocean would snuff out my life in an instant. No mistake about it. No fault of the sea, though. A simple fact that I dared not deny.

Genesis tells us that God looked on all that God had created and proclaimed that it was good – in fact, "very good" (Genesis 1:31). And did not God, after the Great Flood, make a covenant with "every living creature of all flesh that is on the earth" (Genesis 9:16)?

God made a covenant with Bambi and Peter Rabbit – and with the giant saltwater crocodiles of Southeast Asia. I may not like it, or understand it, but all life is of God, all life is good – even saltwater crocodiles.

Did Jesus Christ Save E.T.?

If we discovered that we were not alone in the universe, how would that change our understanding of the salvific role of Jesus Christ? Would we understand Jesus of Nazareth as E.T.'s saviour, or would E.T. have needed an E.T. type of Jesus Christ for his or her – or its –salvation?

In the February 3, 2011, issue of *Nature*, the international weekly journal of science, you will find an article entitled "A Closely Packed System of Low-mass, Low-density Planets Transiting Kepler-11." I'm sure you can't wait to read it. Most articles in *Nature* never get picked up by the media, but this one did.

The Kepler spacecraft was launched by NASA on March 9, 2009. Its mission: to estimate the fraction of sun-like stars that have Earth-like planets. Expressed in a more sensational manner, Kepler's mission is to seek out habitable planets in our Milky Way galaxy.

Named after the German astronomer Johannes Kepler (1571–1630), who worked out the laws of planetary motion, the Kepler mission seeks planets by examining the same fixed field of view over a set period of time – ideally, for the next three to four years. It focuses on 150,000 stars within the Cygnus and Lyra constellations. As a potential planet passes between its sun and the detecting Kepler satellite, the dimming of the sun's light is measured, thus permitting the determination of the planet's radius. The time between planetary transits around its sun permits the determination of the planet's orbital period.

To date, a little over 1,200 candidate planets have been discovered in our galaxy. Of these 1,200-plus planets, sixty-eight are approximately Earth-sized.

The *Nature* article describes the discovery of a solar system, dubbed Kepler-11, that has at least six planets orbiting their sun with orbital periods of 10, 13, 22, 31, 46 and 118 days, and masses between 2.3 and more than 300 times that of Earth.

For ages, we have wondered about the uniqueness of Earth. Fiction and film have abounded with images of those little green Martians. UFOs continue to feed our imagination.

The question of whether we are alone in the universe will continue to intrigue us. If we do indeed discover sentient life on some faraway planet in some remote solar system of the universe, our theology will necessarily be challenged – just as it was challenged by the Copernican and Darwinian revolutions. But the God of carbon-based life that we call humanity will just as certainly be the God of silicon-based life or the God of arsenic-based life. God will continue to be God, creator of all that is seen and unseen. It's our notion of God that will need to change.

MAY

Body of Christ

W hat did Jesus look like? Tall or lean? Short or pudgy? Was his nose crooked or straight? The Gospels are mute on the physical appearance of Jesus.

Strange, when you think of it, that the one person who started a global movement like no other has left us no bodily image (*pace*, the Shroud of Turin). Why did the disciples not care to create a picture, carving or image of their Lord and saviour?

Regardless of the absence of any hint of the physical constitution of Jesus Christ, the notion of the Body of Christ is central to Christian iconography.

Christianity has to be the most earthy, the most bodily, of all religions.

We know the all-powerful God, the all-knowing God, through the flesh and blood of the incarnate Jesus Christ. God is known by God's flesh. *Carnus*, the Latin word for "flesh," is the root of the incarnation of God – chili con carne, carnivore, carnal desires, carnival ...

After centuries of debate, the Church understood Jesus Christ as true God *and* true man. Maybe they simply equivocated, refusing to come down on one side or the other. Or maybe they came to see that notions of body and flesh are fundamental to our understanding of God.

For the most part, we get the fact that Jesus was truly divine. As for his humanity, however, we are often less sure of things.

In fact, Karl Rahner, SJ, has suggested that most Christians are probably "crypto-monophysites." In other words, when it comes down to it, most of us live as if Christ has only one nature: his divine nature. We emphasize divinity at the expense of humanity. On the other hand, some Christians have taken just the opposite perspective and emphasized the humanity of Christ at the expense of his divinity.

The beauty of Christian theology, however, is its universal or catholic character. It's never "either/or," but rather "both/and."

The "both/and" approach is also helpful when we talk of the resurrection of Jesus Christ.

Scripture is a constant witness to the resurrection of the full person of Jesus Christ – body and soul, if you will. What the resurrected state really means, I am not able to say. Nor can anyone else, for that matter.

But one thing is obvious. The resurrected Christ is the wounded Christ. To his astonished disciples, Jesus says, "Touch me and see; for a ghost does not have flesh and bones as you see that I have" (Luke 24:39). The resurrected Christ walked with his disciples, appeared to them, ate breakfast with them.

All this to say, I think, that in and through the resurrection of Jesus Christ, the human body – indeed, all matter and everything in creation – is transformed in the loving, eternal embrace of God, the Giver of Life. And that includes everything – body and all.

Why Is the World Green?

I love the forest in the spring.

Every nook and cranny pulses life. Delicate herbs are brightly flowered, taking advantage of the leafless forest canopy, straining the gaining light as the sun moves higher in the spring sky. Shrub tips flicker with the tantalizing tenderness of new growth. Even the ancient cedar stumps, slumping into the forest floor, are dappled with brilliant ephemeral mushrooms poking through the spongy remains of the former forest denizens. Everything is green.

Why are plants green? An obvious answer is that leaves and plants are green because they contain chlorophyll.

Chlorophyll is the basis of all life on the planet. At a point in Earth history, an organism evolved that gained the capacity to produce its own food. No need to worry about the next meal. Just sit there, rooted in the moist soil, with leaves outstretched – biological solar panels. Mix in some carbon dioxide and water with the energy from the sun, stir in a few odds and ends, and voilà, instant food. This photosynthesis is a marvellous evolutionary invention. A "waste product" of photosynthesis is oxygen, the basis of all aerobic life on the planet, including you and me.

Chlorophyll works best by absorbing most light in the blue and red wavelengths of the so-called electromagnetic spectrum. Chlorophyll is not so good at absorbing light in the green portion of the spectrum. This wavelength of light is reflected, not absorbed by the leaf, which is the real reason that plants are green.

Magnesium is hidden in the midst of the chlorophyll molecule. Magnesium regulates the fixation of carbon in the production of carbohydrates. Even plants need good nutrition.

I remember well the strain of understanding – and remembering – the complexity of photosynthesis as a first-year forestry student. I've forgotten most of the details – but the wonder of it all has never left me. Life was warmed into existence by the rays of the sun. The cauldron of life boiled over. Atmospheric oxygen levels increased and aerobic life blossomed.

In the first chapter of the Book of Genesis, we read that God made the light and the waters on the first two days. Plants were created on the third day. Not till the sixth day were humans created. It seems that the ancient author of Genesis intuited what we know today. Plants are the basis for all else. That's why humans had to wait for the sixth day. We are dependent on the chlorophyll molecule.

So, the next time you find yourself wondering why the world is green, just get down on one knee and give thanks for all the plants that have gone before. They have given us life.

This Is the Cup of My Blood

I cannot imagine the northern forests without them. Each spring, across the far-flung expanse of spruce, fir and pine, they emerge by the millions. From their aquatic wombs, out they pop. To flight they take, intent on only one thing – blood. Warm human blood, in particular.

Shortly after arriving back east one year, I joined my family for a Victoria Day lunch at the cabin. It wasn't long before most of the family had retreated indoors. Swarm after swarm of blackflies emerged from the spring forests, warmed into life by the rising sun.

The blackfly, *la mouche noire*, is one of over 1800 species of blackflies worldwide. Strong men (and women, too, I imagine), have gone crazy because of these insects, they say. No body orifice is small enough to stop the relentless assault. Eyes, ears, nose, scalp and throat are prime targets for the little beasties intent on drawing blood needed for the nourishment of their young. A strong anticoagulant prevents the blood from clotting during the blackflies' feeding. Nice.

Only the female blackfly bites. But try and distinguish male from female as hordes divebomb every square centimetre of skin.

"Take this, all of you and drink from it, for this is the chalice of my Blood, the Blood of the new and eternal covenant, which will be poured out for you and for many for the forgiveness of sins. Do this in memory of me" (Words of Institution, Roman Rite Eucharistic Prayer).

A blood sacrifice is central to Christian iconography. Jesus Christ is the sacrifice, the Paschal Lamb, the One who shed his blood so that we may live. It's not the only image of Christ, but central, nonetheless.

Foundation of the Eucharist, witness of martyrs, liberation from our prison of sin, the sacrifice of Christ runs deep and strong within us.

Each spring and early summer, I don't mind offering up some of my blood for the blackfly so that it may live. Maybe it will be the most Christ-like act I will make.

If ever the blackfly failed to emerge, I would begin to worry. The clean boreal waters birth the blackfly, the forests buzz with life, the brook trout rise to gorge after the winter fast, and I venture forth into the freshness of green.

Love for Those Common Things

I came across *Taraxacum officinale* for the first time the other day. You may know it as "piss-the-bed." At least that's what we called them in Newfoundland. Our francophone neighbours on the islands of St. Pierre and Miquelon used the French colloquial *pissenlit*. The term "dandelion" is probably most familiar. Dandelion is a corruption of the French *dent de lion* (lion's tooth), referring to the angular, tooth-shaped leaves growing as a whorl at the base of the flowering stem.

As youngsters we picked the dandelion leaves for our parents, who would prepare delicious meals of cooked "greens" with
dinner. Many an entrepreneurial kid would be found hawking
bags of "greens" plucked from the roadsides and alleyways.
Dandelion wine was left to the more adventuresome. During a
wilderness survival course taken during my philosophy studies
(I know, it does sound strange), we used the flower heads in
a pancake breakfast after a night shivering in our hand-made
shelters of sticks and stones. High protein value, proclaimed our
instructor. Definitely overrated.

You may think that the flower head is but one single flower.
You would, of course, be mistaken. That bright yellow head is actually made of many small flowers, called florets. The dandelion
is in the family of flowering plants called *Asteraceae* (star-like)
or *Compositae*. *Compositae* describes well the many-flowered
composite characteristic of the dandelion and the more than
22,500 species in the aster, daisy or sunflower family.

There are two types of florets: disc florets and ray florets.
The inner portion of the flower head or capitulum is comprised
of florets with tubular corollas; these are the disc florets, and
they represent the "centre" of the flower. The outer, more showy
portion of the capitulum is comprised of florets with a single
strap-like petal; these are the ray florets, and they represent the
"petals" of the flower. The composition of *Compositae* flower
heads can range from all ray flowers, as in the case of dandelions,
to all disc flowers, as in the case of thistles.

I used to love squeezing out the milky white latex from the
dandelion stem. During the Second World War, the Russian
dandelion (*Taraxacum koksaghyz*), a Slavic cousin of our dandelion, was used as a source of rubber. The roots of the Russian
dandelion contain large amounts of the juicy latex. Interest in

such dandelion-based rubber has grown in light of a fungus that is threatening the rubber trees of Southeast Asia.

At the end of their flowering, the dandelion forms, as you know, those delicate spherical globes of seeds or achenes attached to their own little parachute. An ingenious way to spread their genes. Let the wind whisper and off they go in all directions. How I loved to aid such seed dispersal with the slightest of breath, just like the breath of the Holy Spirit, the giver of life.

The common dandelion has become just that – common. Native to Eurasia, *Taraxacum officinale* has spread to all the world. Some consider it a weed. For others, it's an evolutionary success story, as it disperses and establishes itself with facility and ease.

We often take little interest in common things – like dandelions, starlings and crows. Familiarity breeds contempt, we say. Even the Latin epithet *vulgaris*, often used for such common species, betrays our mild contempt for the "vulgar," or at least a recognition of their commonness. Think of the lowly beet (*Beta vulgaris*), the lilac tree (*Syringa vulgaris*) or the starling (*Sturnus vulgaris*), that most ubiquitous of city birds.

For some reason, however, I have always been attracted by dandelions. Maybe yellow is my colour. Maybe I like the fact that you're always sure to find a dandelion or two in flower, except during the dead of winter. And the fact that they grow in so-called waste spaces helps to brighten what could otherwise be a drab sort of place.

So, the next time you decide to engage in mechanical or chemical warfare on those dandelions, why not give them a second look? The fact that they're so "weedy" means that they have evolved some remarkable life skills. Take a look at their flowers – fascinating, actually. And think of those bright, breezy days when the air is alive with the fecundity of dandelion parachutes.

If that does not enkindle attraction in your heart, you can always boil them up for a good feed of greens. Local, organic and nutritious – what more could you ask for?

God on the Mountain

A web-based ad by Newfoundland and Labrador Tourism pans down through the magnificent fjord of Western Brook Pond in Gros Morne National Park on Newfoundland's west coast. The scrolling caption reads: "The world can't weigh you down when you're standing on top of it."

Maybe that's why I head off to the mountains whenever I can. Not long ago, I accompanied a buddy of mine on a hike to Coliseum Mountain in Lynn Headwaters Regional Park in Vancouver. He was offering a hike in the name of the Alpine Club of Canada, so my friend wanted to do a day of reconnaissance. Of course, I immediately accepted and committed myself to the 10-hour, 20-kilometre hike with a 1,200-metre elevation gain.

During a recent retreat in Abbotsford, I crossed the border one day and drove to Mount Baker-Snoqualmie National Forest to admire up close the snow-covered glaciated volcano of Mount Baker under blazing blue skies. I wanted to set up tent and rest a while. It was simply stunning, and I promised myself a return visit.

What is it about mountains that "peak" our attention? Many things, I suppose. Mountains are the home of the gods (and God), the purveyors of the sublime and guardians of mystery. Mountains attract countless climbers and hikers. What would Canada be without the Rockies? Jesus of Nazareth preached the "sermon on the mount." Moses received the Ten Commandments on Mount Sinai. Benedictines prefer to build their monasteries on mountains. Many a hiker grinds up Grouse Mountain in Vancouver each day.

We see far from mountains. There's nothing above us to worry about. It takes effort to reach the top, but the sacrifices always seem worthwhile. My hiking buddy made a wise statement about mountains, I thought. He said that mountains are always approached slowly and deliberately. One does not climb a mountain in haste. Mountains take time. Respect is demanded. Maybe that is a good paradigm for the spiritual life. Wisdom takes time. Rome was not built in a day. Neither are our lives.

So, the next time you feel weighed down, take to the hills. However, if you must stay on the flats, remember that the road to God is also a great climb – a climb upon which all of us are invited to venture. Despite the many dead ends, one-way streets and wrong turns, the mountain of God will always be there, shrouded in mystery, forever calling us home.

JUNE

Arethusa bulbosa and a Mother

t fifty-three years of age, I still bring wildflowers home to my mom.

It's a strange admission, something not normally shared in print. Most men my age are busy building the world or building their career.

It has been observed that religious life and the vows of poverty, chastity and obedience can stunt a person's psychological growth. I have seen it happen. Adult men and women not sure of their lives, their initiative and sense of responsibility smothered by a false notion of obedience; men and women cold and aloof, bothered by a twisted celibacy or chastity; men and women oblivious to the material dimensions of life.

As I made my way across the bog with the prized bog orchid in hand, thoughts of "acting one's age" couldn't have been further from my mind. I was simply intent on delighting my mom with the beauty of the Dragon Mouth, one of the most beautiful orchids in the North American flora.

To botanists, the Dragon Mouth (or swamp pink) goes by the Latin binomial *Arethusa bulbosa* L. Named after the beautiful Greek nymph Arethusa, the orchid adorns the wet, acidic Sphagnum bogs of Newfoundland in late June and early July.

It's considered rare throughout its range in eastern North America, but in Newfoundland it's a rather common blessing. In fact, the bog I crossed seemed chock full of the pink beauty with its floral configuration akin to a flaming dragon's mouth.

Keeping it secure in its spongy Sphagnum home, I selected one for Mom's table at the cabin where I was heading.

Mom tells me that, as a young boy, I always brought her wildflowers after a day of fishing or simply meandering in the woods. It seems to have been a common trait among all my siblings. A genetic blessing.

We delighted in the delight of our mother when she saw us return from our wanderings, our hands stuffed with dangling bouquets of yellow buttercups and dandelions, blue violets, red wild roses – and purple thistles or knotweed when pickings were slim.

I know I'm not immune to the hazards of the vows of religion. They can be quite dangerous to the unaware. However, they can also gift a person with life. They can help a person focus on what's really important – the now, the "naked now," as Richard Rohr, OFM, is fond of saying.

While crossing that bog last week, the naked now spoke of the delight that *Arethusa bulbosa* would bring to my mom.

Delight always elicits delight. Gift rendered is gift received. Maybe that's why, at fifty-three years of age, I still pick wildflowers for my mother. At fifty-three, I still need to know the pleasure of delight – delight given and delight received.

Galaxies and God: Thumbs Up and Thumbs Down

With the help of the Hubble telescope, a team of astronomers has discovered what they say is the earliest galaxy ever glimpsed in the heavens. A smudge of galactic light on a Hubble image clocks in at a mere 480 million years after the Big Bang – light from a fledgling galaxy 13.3 billion years ago.

That story is wondrous enough. More intriguing, however, were the comments posted on the CBC website that announced the stellar news. One early commentator weighed in with the following response: "In the beginning, God created the heavens and the earth. It's an amazing discovery – looking at the very beginning of God's work."

What surprised me was the next comment. It was soon removed by the moderator of the site. This comes as no surprise, given that the writer, in strident, self-righteous anger, thundered what the *&?$ this nonsense was all about. God has nothing to do with this story, and besides, all priests and bishops are pedophiles and when are we going to grow up and move beyond such infantile and asinine thinking. The author ended the diatribe with an emphatic "Frigg!!!!" One other commentator stated that the discovery shows that "science rules," while another assuredly noted that "secular society rules" and that "it will be the future of man."

In case you're wondering, the "God" listing, at last count, had received nineteen "thumbs up" – and 184 "thumbs down." The energetic riposte, on the other hand, had garnered just the opposite – 194 "thumbs up" and only four "thumbs down."

I admit that anonymous responses to Internet news stories are not the best sources of civil or reasoned discourse. However, they do suggest a certain public mood.

I can calmly read the God statement and appreciate its content. The Christian doctrine of creation welcomes this scientific discovery. Creation, as a theological notion, is not fully encompassed by the "how" of the origins of the universe.

The person commenting on God as Creator seemed to think the same, given his or her amazement at the discovery of this early galaxy. His or her mind was open and flexible enough to absorb the wonder of science and the mystery of God at the same time. For the respondent, however, such seemed not the case. Missing was an openness to multiple layers of explanation where faith and science could learn from each other.

We seem to be slipping into what we could call a "poverty of discourse." The world is no longer complex and mysterious, a wonder to behold. Rather, lines are being drawn in the sand. We're on the hunt for who's in and who's out. Our world is shrinking to fit our minds – and in the process we truncate the rich variety and stuff of life.

There is only one world. For some reason, however, we seem increasingly unable to embrace the varied textures and depths of our world. Content with the superficial, we resist the depths of the deep. Easy and quick answers abound. Our refusal to ask all the needed questions is a precursor to a cycle of decline. Let us never shrink from questions. They are the foundations of faith.

Eucharist on the MV *Kouju Lily*

I looked at my watch. It was just after midnight. She'd now be on her way, I thought. I wished her a safe journey as she slipped under the Lions Gate Bridge in Vancouver, down the Straits of Georgia to the open Pacific.

When I checked several days later on the Internet, the MV *Kouju Lily* was located just northwest of San Francisco, sailing at 12.7 knots on a bearing of 161 degrees. She had left Vancouver with her hold full of Prairie grain. Her destination: the Mexican deepwater port of Veracruz on the Atlantic Coast. Then on to Europe for the next leg of her journey.

I celebrated the Eucharist on board the *Kouju Lily* several hours before it departed. The day before, its crew of twenty, all Filipino, had requested Mass. Since the Catholic port chaplain was not available, I was asked to fill in. I gladly accepted.

The mess hall table was adorned with a clean, fresh linen tablecloth. The small mess hall had been transformed into a floating chapel. The crew's dining table became the altar of sacrifice and the table of communion.

Something amazing about the Eucharist. Here we were, meeting for the first time, coming from different parts of the world, different cultures, different native tongues, and yet united as members of the one Body of Christ. We prayed for family, for safety at sea. The bread and wine became for us all the Body and Blood of Christ. We ate and drank together.

Their journey would continue to take them across the seas of the world, eight months at a time. My journey took me back to Point Grey, to St. Mark's College at the University of British Columbia.

That night, as I lay asleep on the Endowment Lands, the crew of the *Kouju Lily* would have maneuvered their 58,000-tonne bulk carrier around the waters of Point Grey on their way south to the Panama Canal.

I remembered their faces, their generosity, their warmth. I left them some holy cards and other religious objects, blessed during the Mass. The remaining items were taken for their families back home. They generously helped me clean up and left me several envelopes stuffed with American bills.

I may never again meet the captain and crew of the *Kouju Lily*. And yet I can check their position at sea via the Internet anytime I want. The Mass created a bond, I think. We all professed the one Lord Jesus Christ. We all knew of our need for God – and ultimately for each other.

I suspect that I will never look at the waiting freighters in the waters off Vancouver's Spanish Banks in the same way as before. No longer will they simply be ships waiting to be loaded with grain or coal. This time, they'll have acquired more of a human face. Ships peopled by the crews of the merchant marine.

In particular, I will remember that small crew of the MV *Kouju Lily* with whom I shared the Body and Blood of Christ. We ate of the same bread and shared the same cup. That makes us brothers, friends in the Lord, I suppose. Godspeed – and *bon voyage*.

Avatar

I finally saw the movie *Avatar* more than four months after its release. The movie could still draw a crowd. Early headlines focused on the Vatican's supposed critique of the film for its spiritualism linked to the worship of nature. It's funny how a review by a lone film critic can be inflated to "the Vatican." But that's another story.

As for the claim of nature worship, that seemed to miss the point, in my opinion. Even Christianity has the Tree of Life as its central icon. Jesus was crucified on a tree that becomes the source of life and blessing in and through the resurrection. Nature is central to human salvation. Nature is sacramental, revelatory of God. That's not nature worship. That's simply good Catholic theology.

What struck me, rather, was the vision of humanity portrayed in the film. I left the film dissipated. The film seemed "hope-less." The rich, textured complexities of human–nature interactions were reduced to the simplistic dichotomy of evil versus good – the evil, greedy, rapacious industrial-military complex on the one side opposed to the good, harmonious, nature-based, communitarian life of the Na'vi on the other side. The human is evil. The non-human is good. The only way to resolve the issue was a clash of firepower.

The hero, Jake Sully, must cease to be human to save the day. Humanity is irredeemable, inherently flawed and destitute. Only by becoming an "avatar," something other than human, is the day saved.

When I emerged from the film, it was not into the forest paths of Pandora that I stepped, but rather into the lighted, asphalted streets of Earth, surrounded not by the Na'vi, but by fellow humans. This is where the drama is played out. Not on some other world, but here on this Earth we call home, this Earth that is a complex of languages, cultures, religions, political and economic systems. This is where the new struggle is waged. Never before in human or Earth history have we been faced with the dilemma of how to live with the rest of nature.

I think this realization frightens us. We cry out with a loud lament. We shrink in fear before our power and responsibility. We are crippled by our actions that seem to know no respect or boundaries.

For me, *Avatar* did not fall into nature worship, but something much more troubling – a misanthropic flight from the world. That's tempting, I know. However, something more is needed.

There is only one world. We are not avatars. We are human, born of the stuff of the earth (humus), and called to share in the divine life of God. Like the Tree of Life, we are rooted in Earth and we reach out to Heaven. It is in the tension of this blessed human vocation that solutions are sought.

Lichens and Men of the Cloth

Before arriving at St. Mark's College (Vancouver, BC) in 2009, I worked with the Wildlife Division of the Newfoundland and Labrador Department of Environment and Conservation. I managed a survey of rare lichens in the forests of eastern Newfoundland. In the winter of 2009, I spent a week at the lichen herbarium of the New Brunswick Museum in Saint John.

One day, while perusing the lichen collection, I came across a series of lichens collected in 1943 by two Roman Catholic priests: Rev. Arthème Dutilly, OMI (1896–1973), naturalist of the Oblate Arctic Missions, and Rev. Ernest Lepage (1885–1981) of the École d'Agriculture in Rimouski, Quebec.

Being a devotee of botany and lichenology, it was with great interest that I delved into the lives of these two priests.

Between 1943 and 1963, both priests collaborated on several botanical expeditions into the boreal forests and tundra of northern Quebec. Over a twenty-year period, they canoed a total of 7,500 kilometres throughout the northern reaches, collected plants, mosses and lichens, and published extensively.

Rev. Dutilly became the director of the Arctic Institute at the Catholic University of America. He is the eponym of a northern dwarf birch, *Betula x dutillyi Lepage*, among other plant species.

Rev. Lepage is considered one of the great pioneers of Canadian botany. He named 173 new plant names or taxa and published over 100 botanical papers in peer-reviewed journals. His personal herbarium of up to 35,000 plants eventually found a home at Université Laval's Herbier Louis-Marie.

Both men follow in the great botanical tradition of Brother Marie-Victorin (1885–1944), a de la Salle Christian Brother, founder of the Botanical Gardens of Montreal and author of the masterpiece *Flore laurentienne* (1935), a record of the entire flora of southern Quebec.

Another priest, Rev. Léon Abel Provancher (1820–1892) was the founder, in 1868, of *Le naturaliste canadien*, a scientific journal that still exists today. He is considered the father of Canadian natural history.

So, my love for those lichens is not unusual for "men of the cloth." In the Creed, we profess faith in Jesus Christ "through whom all things were made" – all things, even lichens.

JULY

Home Sweet Home

As Jesuit novices, we used to spend time at a small Jesuit villa (cottage) in the lovely country town of Belfountain, not far from the novitiate in Guelph, Ontario.

Close to Belfountain flow the upper reaches of the Credit River. Close to its source, the Credit runs free and cold and supports a healthy run of brook trout.

Along one section of the Credit River are several houses. Nestled near the river, bounded by the rich, forested slopes on the far side of the river valley, these homes always attracted me. One house in particular always caught my attention. From a ground-level window of this particular house emanated a soft glow of light. Each time I walked by the house in the cool of the fall evening, the warm light tugged at my heart.

At the time, I could not name the reason for such attraction. I was having a difficult time as a novice. For some reason, the lighted windows secured me. Only now can I see what was happening. I was longing for home. I was not homesick in the normal sense of the term, but I was certainly agitated at a much deeper level.

The glowing windows spoke of the safety and solace of home and hearth. As I peered through the windows from a distance, I imagined a safe and reassuring world beyond the panes. Beyond the windows lay a world that I had somehow forsaken – the world of home, hearth and family.

One summer, the road was my home. New Brunswick, Maine, Newfoundland, Kenya, Germany, Finland, back to Newfoundland, on to Ontario – and finally British Columbia. As I write, I'm living in a lovely cabin in the woods of northeast Maine, complete with heat, lights and hot running water. It's my home for now.

I sometimes feel the pain of no fixed address. Moving and transitions are not easy for me. Sometimes, greater stability seems sweetly attractive, vows of monastic stability seem downright reasonable, and the celibate life downright questionable.

But, for some reason, I seem to have found a home no matter where time has taken me. Given my predilection for home and hearth, I don't understand this.

Call it grace, or simply luck, but the world seems to have become my home. Time and experience have proved that I am sustained by a Love that holds me, protects me and blesses me in ways unimaginable. I say goodbye to some people only to be welcomed by others. I find a mountain to climb, a favourite place to walk, a quiet place to find peace. It may take a while, but eventually home somehow finds me.

To be "at home." I suppose it's something we all long for. We try to build it. We attempt to create it. We may even try to steal it. Regardless, I think that we all long to "come home."

Given my Jesuit life, a life often marked by itinerancy and solitude, I find that "home" is never really created but rather is given as a gift. It's grace.

So, while I may never have a beautiful, familiar home reminiscent of the one from my novitiate walks along the banks of the Credit River, I have come to be at home wherever life has taken me. Thanks be to God for that.

At Home in the Fog

The land finally succumbed. Resistance had weakened in the cool of the evening. Nothing could stop it now. Slowly, quietly, in the hush of dusk, it crept landward, draping the headlands in its cool, moist embrace. Funnelling up harbours and valleys, wafting through open windows, shrouding all in silence, it advanced, relentlessly. The darkened land would now sleep, blanketed in the shroud of night.

I think that fog lives in my bones. For sure, it lives in my heart and soul. I happened to be born not far from the confluence of those two great Atlantic arteries – the Gulf Stream and the Labrador Current. Their intercourse spawns the best fog in the world.

The Gulf Stream transports warm waters from the tip of Florida, along the Atlantic Seaboard, out past Newfoundland on its way across the Atlantic to western and northern Europe. Over 100 kilometres wide and a kilometre deep, it cruises along, pushing over 150 million cubic metres per second as it passes south of Newfoundland.

Running south in the opposite direction is the cold Labrador current, transporting frigid waters from the high Arctic, along the Labrador coast and around Newfoundland. That cold tongue of life escorts the countless icebergs calving off the heights of Greenland to create Newfoundland's "iceberg alley." And with the ice come the millions of harp seals, giving birth on the solid pans of sea ice. The polar bears follow, gorging on the feast.

On the Grand Banks, the tongues of cold and warm kiss, generating the well-known summer fogs of Newfoundland and the north Atlantic. The arrival of the wet, cold fog signals what we call "capelin weather," that time of early summer when millions of silvered capelin roll upon Newfoundland beaches in an orgy of sperm and egg.

Humpback whales follow the capelin on their journey north to feed in the rich, cold waters. Ever smell the "burp" of a humpback? One such burp from a humpback almost knocked me off my feet, so strong was the stench of partially digested capelin.

Each day welcomes the rising eastern sun that slowly eats away at the marauding fog. Beaten back by the steady, warm gaze, the fog retreats seaward, letting the land once again have its day in the sun.

But the fog does not go far. Only a kilometre or so, out on the water, far enough away from the deadly heat of the land, the mammoth fog banks brood, patiently biding their time when they may again advance and reclaim the land. And wait they will, if the wind is right. The land can resist only for so long. The cool of the evening will again fall upon the land – and the daily tug of war will continue.

Sometimes, advancing strands of fog attempt to pierce the barrier of heat simmering over the land. Scouts of fog foray forth, advance in earnest, only to be beaten back under a phalanx of solar defence. But they know that their time will come, especially as the days of summer advance and the sun loses its grip upon the land.

A difference of 5 degrees Celsius can mark one end of St. John's from the other. We always called late summer (after the first of August) "sweater weather." A good friend likes to quip that Newfoundland has two seasons – winter and August. Not exactly true, though not far from it. Coastal fog does much to command the weather of southeastern Newfoundland.

We are defined by the nature that surrounds us. Fog defines southeastern Newfoundland. We may curse it. We may love it. Let the foghorns wail and the whales rejoice.

Stained Glass in the Morning

As I waited in the early morning chapel for the beginning of Mass, the stained glass caught the first rays of the morning sun. The darkness now gleamed with the warmed filtered light.

The rectangular and angular slices of glass transformed the incoming sun into a kaleidoscope of colour. My gaze rested on the soft, warm glow streaming in from outside.

Visible light comprises a small subset of the full spectrum of electromagnetic radiation. To be exact, visible light has a wavelength of between approximately 400 and 700 nanometres. We can't see ultraviolet light (shorter than 400 nm) or infrared light (longer than 700 nm).

As you know, there is more to visible light than meets the eye. Rainbows reveal the inner life of visible light, showing off the range of colour from red to violet. For some reason, I remember well the mnemonic "Robert of York gained battle in vain," which helped me to remember the seven colours of the rainbow – red, orange, yellow, green, blue, indigo and violet.

Just as the rainbow reveals the inner life of visible light, stained glass may be said to reveal the inner life of the invisible God. Only in the presence of light does the stained glass glow in truth and meaning. Almost like the grace of God that enlightens our mind, heart and soul.

My focus on the streaming warm light through the chapel's glass ended abruptly when the sacristan entered to prepare for Mass. On came the lights, jarring in their artificiality. Their bright shrillness overshadowed the soft emanations of the stained glass. It was like turning off the stained glass. All that remained were coloured pieces of glass that had lost their spark of life. Their heartbeat has ceased.

In Leonard Cohen's celebrated song "Anthem," he has a line that goes like this: "There is a crack, a crack in everything. That's how the light gets in."

The glory of the stained glass was manifest only in the early morning darkness of the chapel. The darkness glorified the sunlight as it shone through the stained glass. Once the chapel was brightened by its own light, the glory of the stained glass withered and retreated from sight. The sunlight still shone through, but its effect was no longer felt.

Our lives and the life of the world can sometimes feel like that. We may often "feel" God's absence. But when it comes to the grace of God, feelings have little to tell. The light of God's grace is constant and forever. In fact, there is no such thing as pure nature. Nature is "by nature" spirited nature. All of creation is "ensouled," enlivened by the grace of God.

We may not be aware of God's constant showering of grace. But that doesn't mean it does not exist. Only the rainbow reveals the hidden beauty of visible light. Only the inner darkness of a small chapel enabled its stained glass to glory in the light of the morning sun. Only the "cracks" of humility and of poverty of spirit enable the glory of God to be revealed and experienced.

So, the next time you fret over the "absence" of God, think of the inner beauty of light as given by the rainbow. Reflect on stained glass that works only when the inside is dark. And rest in the wisdom of Leonard Cohen, who rightly noted that the cracks and failures of our lives permit the abundant grace of God to pour unreservedly into the depths of our soul.

Spirituality of Forests

The contemporary refrain of protest against the loss of global forests speaks something more fundamental, more central than that encompassed by standard environmental impact statements. I sense that we are reacting on a more visceral level to a sense of loss that is difficult to grasp, probably impossible to measure, but nonetheless real at a most basic level.

We gaze upon creation and witness the loss and death we have unleashed. We witness the loss of beauty, of countless images and experiences provided by the diversity of forests and wild places. As the trees fall and the hills are laid bare, our human hearts, both individual and collective, are pierced. As forests are destroyed and species and wilderness are lost, no less is the diminishment of the human spirit. Global deforestation spawns a culture of death, which no longer recognizes the divinely inspired contemplative gaze upon creation. A culture of death that kills both our physical needs for survival as well as our aesthetic and spiritual sensibilities. A denuded landscape and a diminished human spirit become one and the same.

I wonder if the source of our lament (about the loss of forests and wild places) is rooted in the acknowledgement, be it explicit or unconscious, that our current rapacious relationship with the world's forests is inherently dehumanizing and contrary to the human spirit. In our seemingly relentless ravaging of the world's forests, we have failed to acknowledge that forests are not simply "natural," but in fact a creative response of divine Love. We have failed to acknowledge that our forested world, indeed all of nature, may be more than it seems; that it may speak of divine beauty and love in and through its myriad sights, sounds and wonders. Consequently, we have assumed a power that reduces our natural world to superficial matter, meaningless and inchoate. Such a perspective breeds covetousness and a grasping greed. This pernicious exercise of power is seductive and effectively blinds us to the essential sacramental heart of nature.

Global deforestation and loss of primary forests is paradigmatic of our need for an "ecological conversion." For only authentic religious, moral and intellectual conversion will gift us with the eyes to see and the ears to hear. The eyes to see and the ears to hear the Blessed Trinity at the heart of creation. The Blessed Trinity, creator of all that is seen and unseen. The Blessed Trinity, through whom all things were made. The Blessed Trinity, the giver of life.

Silence

Several years ago, I did an eight-day retreat with other Jesuits and some colleagues at the Manresa Jesuit Spiritual Renewal Centre in Pickering, Ontario.

It was a silent retreat, as are all such retreats.

Silence is a strange thing. It's something that we both resist and crave.

We all have responsibilities and jobs and projects that demand the opposite of silence – raising children, taking classes, working, living in family or community. Humans live by language and words. Books, Internet, chat rooms, e-mail, TV, video, song, literature, Facebook, Twitter, Skype, and simple heart-to-heart conversation. Without words and language, we die.

In this cacophonous world, however, there is another voice that longs to be heard. It is the voice hidden deep within that whispers, "Be still, and know that I am God" (Psalm 46:10). For reasons often unknown, we resist this interior call to silence. It's no wonder. The entry into the interior life can be a treacherous journey. All kinds of demons and bogeymen lie in wait for the unwary traveller. But, strangely enough, there is no other way.

Pull yourself away to silence and you may be introduced to your own demons, who are often, as Scripture says, legion

(Luke 8:30). The many voices of regret, fear, sin and anxiety. The voices of things said and done. The voices of things unsaid and undone.

But the only way into life is in and through the silent life. Jesus understood this. Before he began his public life, Scripture says, he was drawn into the wilderness by the Spirit, where he was tempted by the devil (Matthew 4:1). Throughout his entire life, Jesus would withdraw into the mountains, to a deserted place, to pray. Even in his final hour, he would be drawn into the silence of the Garden of Gethsemane, where he waged the final struggle with himself. Jesus knew the power of silence.

Wilderness is the biblical symbol for the inner, silent life. The Exodus story is a story of liberation from slavery, through the crucible of forty years of temptation, depravation and fear in the wilderness, through the chaos of the Red Sea, into the promised land flowing with milk and honey. This is the paradigm of the spiritual life. The dying and rising to new life. The Paschal Mystery of Jesus Christ is our paschal mystery.

We all need to create a place and time of silence in our lives. Prayer does exactly that. Prayer invites us into the wilderness, into the silence of our hearts, so that we may attune ourselves to the whispers of God.

Remember the meeting of the prophet Elijah with God on Mount Horeb. God was not found in the great wind, nor in the earthquake, nor in the fire. Only when Elijah heard the "sound of sheer silence" (1 Kings 19:12) did he go out and stand at the entrance of his cave to meet God.

So, be still, and may your silence be filled with the Word of God.

AUGUST

Time in the Torngats

L ook for the Torngat Mountains National Park in the extreme northern regions of Labrador. All above the treeline, the park hosts the highest mountains east of the Rockies and some of the oldest rocks on the planet – up to 3.9 billion years, they say. That's remarkable, considering the age of the Earth is around 4.54 billion years.

Several years ago, I spent eight days in the Torngats. I was there compliments of Parks Canada, which asked me to come to the park, to experience it, and to help tell the story of the park and the people.

No one lives in the park, but it has been the traditional home of the Inuit people of northern Quebec (Nunavik) and northern Labrador (Nunatsiavut). The park is currently managed by a Cooperative Management Board composed of Inuit from both Nunavik and Nunatsiavut. Inuit are permitted to continue their traditional hunting, fishing and gathering in the park. All people who go to the Torngats enter the park at a base camp located just south of the national park boundary.

Nunatsiavut is best translated from Inuktitut as "Our Beautiful Land." Never have I experienced such raw, elemental beauty. Long, deep coastal fjords slice the primeval coast with cliffs towering 900 metres out of the cold Labrador Sea. Our helicopter pilot was well versed as he safely manoeuvred these breathtaking fjords that funnel deadly winds down from the glaciated George Plateau.

The frigid coastal waters abounded in life – bearded and harp seals, minke whales, dolphins, birds of all kinds – and a healthy population of *nanuk*, the white bear of the north. I was awestruck by my first sighting of a large female polar bear with her two cubs scooting over the gentle slopes of a coastal island. Black bears were a common sighting – apparently the only known population of barren-ground black bear. The base camp was protected by an electric fence at night, and armed Inuit bear monitors accompanied us on our travels.

For many, the Torngats is a wilderness landscape. Wilderness it is. Several times I shuddered before the starkness and naked power of the land – a power that I knew could so easily snuff out my life. One does not enter this land without some thought.

For others, particularly the Inuit, the Torngats are a homeland. Hundreds of archaeological sites exist in the park, reminders of occupation over thousands of years by the Maritime Archaic Indians, the Pre-Dorset and Dorset Paleo-Eskimos and the Thule culture, the ancient ancestors of the contemporary Inuit of these northern lands.

I was privileged to help build a rock cairn that welcomed the remains of several Inuit who had been removed from their burial sites by archaeologists in the 1960s. From where we stood, we could see many rocks cairns that served as ancient burial sites of the nomadic Inuit peoples. The polar bears also loved this low-lying, gently sloped island, a fact witnessed by the many seal skeletons that littered the grassy and mossy hollows.

Torngat means "land of the spirits." The word is derived from *Torngarsoak*, the most powerful of the Inuit spirits. Today, the Inuit claim the Christian faith, but there still resides the mighty spiritual powers of the Torngats. I wish I could put words to that spirit. But maybe, as with the Holy Spirit, we are mute before the ineffable. All we can do is offer our lives in prayer and abandon.

Labrador Journey – or
What I Did on My Summer Holidays

Our destination was the Benedict Mountains, a two-hour steam south from Makkovik on the northern Labrador coast. As we approached a long, lonely beach, we saw that we were not alone. A large female bear and her two cubs ambled along the rocky beach – away from us, thankfully. The swell was rising and our guide motioned us to get onto the beach as quickly as we could. Heavy swells would beach the boat, leaving the 75-horsepower engines useless and possibly damaged. Off we plopped onto the beach, enabling our guide to set off safely into deeper and calmer waters. He would meet us several kilometres down the coast at the end of the day.

We had come to collect plants and lichens on this remote northern coast of Labrador – the land that God gave to Cain, according to an early explorer. Our European predecessor must have felt far removed from the tamed pastoral scenes of home. Some of the oldest rocks on the planet come from this part of Labrador, and the cold Labrador current carries so many Greenland icebergs that the locals have named this part of the coast "iceberg alley." That day, under the blazing sun, glacial blue icebergs abounded.

I was part of a botanical expedition sponsored by the Newfoundland and Labrador Wildlife Division and the Atlantic Canada Conservation Data Centre. My job was to collect as many different lichens as I could in the seven days afforded to us.

So many images flood my memory from those few days on the Labrador coast. A mother wolf and her four pups, black bears and their cubs, porpoises, seals, Arctic char that we caught, baked caribou and cloudberry pie for supper, rich productive forests sheltered in the valleys, massive old peaks covered with extensive snowfields in the warm August sun, the solid Canadian shield that determines the landscape … and the quiet, hospitable people, descendants of Inuit and settler ancestry.

What impressed me was the people's intimacy with the land. Our guide carried a rifle and a pump-action shotgun – just in case he saw something interesting. To his credit, he did not pursue a school of porpoises that we encountered one day on the water. His reason? He was on charter with us and did not think it proper to hunt while on the job. We checked Atlantic salmon and Arctic char nets, chipped off some iceberg ice ("bergie bits") to cool down our catch of char, and even landed on a small iceberg to secure some ice for a rum and Coke. Those 10,000-year-old ice cubes gave sparkle to the Jamaican rum.

After our guide picked us up at the end of the day, he said he had seen five more black bear from the water. Obviously, we had companions on our excursion that day. Bear signs were everywhere. I had never seen so many well-used "bear trails" and fresh, abundant bear scat. The bruins had no doubt spied us from a safe distance. We were in their country. They must have known that we were simply friendly visitors out for a pleasant day of lichen hunting.

Male Testes: Intelligent Design or Bad Design?

Why do male testes hang outside the body cavity? If I had a choice in the matter, I would probably have opted for some form of internal design.

Apparently, testes begin to develop in the abdomen, then migrate down into the scrotum outside the body cavity away from the damaging heat of the body just before birth. Sperm, apparently, don't like it too hot.

We've inherited this testicular journey from our fishlike ancestors, whose gonads developed and remained within the abdomen. Our testicular descent was an evolutionary add-on, so to speak.

If we see God as an Intelligent Designer, why couldn't God have done a better job with the male reproductive system? Exposed testes are bad enough. But why run the urethra right through the middle of the prostate gland that produces some of our seminal fluid? Jerry Coyne, in his book *Why Evolution Is True* (2009), described it as having a sewage pipe running through a recreation area.

You may see where I'm going. I don't have too much time for Intelligent Design. Neither do I hold much stock in atheistic evolution. They're both too closed-minded for my liking.

That the entire universe, all of life, and yes, even the male reproductive system, was created by God, I hold dear and true. But that such nature came about through the processes of natural selection, adaptive change, chance and deep time, I also hold dear and true.

God is intimately involved with the world. God is a God of Providence, a God of Love. At the same time, the world possesses its own autonomy. It is "created" after all, and therefore is not divine.

We believe that the universe is the consequence of selfless divine love. Love, by its very nature, lets the other be. If God so loves the world, then maybe God lets the world unfold, not in any predetermined, "designed" manner, but in an open, inviting manner that draws the world forth in myriad expressions of process and pattern. This implies that the world is not finished. It is open to the future, to the "final coming." In the meantime, its 13.8-billion-year story is still unfolding in the love and beauty of God.

As theologian John Haught has noted, proponents of intelligent design and atheistic evolutionary materialism don't go deep enough. The world is not programmed or designed or manipulated by a clockmaker God. Nor is the world empty of God. There exists only one world – the world of scientific explanation *and* the world of divine Providence. In Romans, Saint Paul writes that "creation waits with eager longing ... the whole creation has been groaning in labor pains" (Romans 8:19-22). Listen to Charles Darwin as he writes the final lines of his *On the Origin of Species* (1859): "There is a grandeur in this view of life, with its several powers, having been originally breathed into a few forms or into one; and that whilst this planet has gone cycling on according to the fixed law of gravity, from so simple a beginning, endless forms most beautiful and most wonderful have been, and are being, evolved."

If you listen closely enough, you may hear the same vision of the love and beauty of God.

Saved Together

I am so well aware of how little I really know or understand.

Leafing through some recent issues of *Science* and *Nature* underlines the truth of such awareness. All Greek to me are such titles as "Antidiabetic Actions of a Non-agonist PPAR Ligand Blocking Cdk5-mediated Phosphorylation" or "On-demand Single-electron Transfer between Distant Quantum Dots." Furthermore, I am totally dependent on so many people – be they doctors, mechanics, dentists, pilots, cooks, plumbers or accountants.

I suppose that, one way or another, we're all in the same boat. Our world has become so complicated that no one person, let alone one nation, can ever assume self-sufficiency.

86 DO MONKEYS GO TO HEAVEN?

We need each other.

Teamwork is a *sine qua non* in almost all scientific endeavours. All scientific papers published in *Science* and *Nature* now include a breakdown of who did what in each project. It often takes a large team to conceive the project, design and carry out the experiments, analyze the data and write the manuscript. Author lists citing 50 to 100+ workers from a host of nations and institutions are not uncommon these days. That's one of the beauties of science – it's a corporate effort.

When it comes to salvation, the need for others is even more obvious. At least, that's the theory. So often, however, we think that we can do it alone, that our personal efforts will save the day.

The Church's insistence on weekly attendance at Mass, however, underscores the need for corporate salvation. We're in it together, the poor and the rich, the lame and the strong, the bright and the dull. Believe it or not, we all need each other. We need to hear the mighty "Amen" of the crowd. We need to join others with hands outstretched, longing for the saving body and blood of Jesus Christ.

As a priest, I need to be with others at Sunday Mass. Sure, as a priest, I could celebrate a "private Mass," so to speak, if necessary, but what use is that? Anyway, there is really no such thing as a "private Mass," as all Masses are the work of the Body of Christ. In fact, the Church states that a priest should not celebrate Mass without at least one of the faithful, except for a just and reasonable cause. I remember well, during my early years in the Society of Jesus, large communities with a series of private altars for Jesuits celebrating their daily Mass alone. No wonder people came to joke that there's nothing more useless than a Jesuit priest at Easter.

I am the vine and you are the branches, Jesus says (John 15:5). We are the body of Christ – that perduring image coined by Saint Paul (1 Corinthians 12:12-31; Ephesians 4:1-16).

We're saved together. We pray for each other. We forgive each other. We gather on Sunday one with each other.

So, the next time I get the urge to study the workings of quantum dots and phosphorylation, I will no doubt need a competent team. On my journey in and through God, I'll again call upon a team – a different team, perhaps, but a team nonetheless.

The Anthropocene

We like to classify time and transitions. Geologists are no exception. Beginning in the twentieth century, geologists began to define geological time periods based on the relative position of geological strata and fossils remains.

Our current geological epoch is named the Holocene, a period that began about 11,500 years ago. Human civilization dates entirely within the Holocene. This epoch is marked by the end of the last glacial period and the rise of agriculture, both transitions well defined in the rock and fossil record.

It seems, however, that the Holocene may be no more. Some scientists think we have passed beyond the Holocene and are now living in what is known as the Anthropocene (Age of Humanity). Coined by Nobel prize winner Paul Crutzen in 2000, the term has not yet been formalized, but the debate has begun.

Supporters of the Anthropocene concept claim that the impact of human activity on the environment has reached planetary proportions. In other words, we have passed a new juncture in Earth history where humanity has altered the planet to such an extent that the chemical and biological signal of such change will be discernible thousands of years from now – thus the reasoning that such a change should be formalized with the introduction of a new geological epoch.

Think of all the soil we have moved, the water we have dammed, the forests we have cut, the land we have cleared, the fossil fuels we have burned, the habitats we have transformed. All of these activities have left their mark, their "stratigraphic signal," that will be detectable in the stuff of the earth for generations to come.

Interest in the Anthropocene is growing. The March 2011 issue of *National Geographic* dedicated its cover story to the Anthropocene. Meanwhile, in February 2011, *The New York Times* ran an editorial on the Anthropocene in response to a series of papers published on January 31, 2011, by the Royal Society in England. The editors of this collection of papers, published in the Society's *Philosophical Transactions*, claim that our human impact on the environment "is likely to have significant and long-lasting consequences" and that "the Anthropocene ... seems to show global change consistent with the suggestion that an epoch-scale boundary has been crossed within the last two centuries."

In the beginning, God created the heavens and the earth, creating a cosmos, a home, out of the chaos of the formless void and the darkness over the deep (Genesis 1:1-2). At the other end of the Bible, the sacred writer dreams visions of "a new heaven and a new earth" (Revelation 21:1).

The Bible witnesses to life, to the transformation of chaos into cosmos. The Anthropocene seems ominous – a transformation of cosmos into chaos. It's amazing how things can creep up on you. Come, Holy Spirit, renew the face of the earth!

SEPTEMBER

Beginnings

I like beginnings. Maybe it's my inability to follow through on things! I hope not.

I remember with delight some of the first days of elementary school. The fall goldenrods and thistles of home always nudged me to think ahead to the school year. Change was imminent and I had better get ready. Even the air, with the warmth of summer on the wane, spoke of a new season about to set in.

An early black-and-white photo has me and my three siblings all lined up, fresh brush cuts for the boys, pressed clothes, new book bags, all smiles as we prepared to leave home for the first day of school one September day. I was so proud of my new pencil case filled with sharpened pencils, a ruler and fresh, clean erasers.

The beginning of a new academic year elicits different emotions, I imagine. For some, it's a feverish, dizzying time of everything new. For others, it's the same old, same old. Too many people for some, a joy for others. For some it's downright scary, for others downright delightful.

No matter what, beginnings create a chance for something new.

Each day has a beginning. An obvious and rather mundane statement, I will admit. But I think that we often fail to embrace the significance of the daily beginnings of our days.

We may have difficulty dealing with the present moment. As humans, we bear the heavy cross of the past and the future. So often we live in the past, imprisoned by words said or unsaid, actions done or not done, sins of commission and sins of omission.

In a similar way, the future may hold us in its grip, imprisoning us in unshakeable worry and anxiety.

In the process, we miss the naked now, the only moment we have. The past is gone; let us learn from it. The future is unknown; let us live in hope. All we have is now, this very moment, to be still and know that God is God.

And so, the beginnings of each day are a privileged moment. That is why the monks of the world begin each day with sung morning prayer, and countless men and women of faith start their day with a time of quiet prayer – prayer in the myriad ways known to humanity.

Beginnings – the beginning of a new academic year, the beginning of a life together in marriage, the beginning of a day about to be lived – are a privileged time to stop, wait and listen.

Each day before I rise and put my feet on *terra firma*, I bless myself. I am not a particularly pious person – certainly not in the commonly understood sense of the term. However, the sign of the cross on my body grounds me for a new beginning. My failures, my sin, my fear, my lack of faith, hope and love – all these assume their place within the overarching love of Christ for me and for the world. This a new day, a new beginning. Who knows what the day will bring? Who knows when the waves of redeeming grace will wash over our tired shores and call us to new life?

A new semester, a new day … a new beginning.

Moses and the Hitchhiker

On the cardboard sign strung over his neck were the words "Argentia ferry." With a pack on his back, his thumb was out for the ride. Without hesitation, I pulled over and waited for him. Up he ran, stuffed his gear into the back seat and jumped in.

Well tanned from days under the sun, tattoos along his arms, a black baseball cap on his head, he greeted me amiably. For some reason, I liked him from the start.

I don't often pick up hitchhikers. At least, not with all the stories one hears these days. But sometimes, I just have a sense. The road he was on was not well travelled. No one hitchhikes that road. And he was going in the right direction for the Nova Scotia ferry.

He was from the South Shore of Nova Scotia. It was his first time in Newfoundland. For the past week he had travelled the roads of the Avalon Peninsula, mostly on foot. He was now on his way back home. A friend in Cape Breton and a sister in Halifax would round off his visiting before his journey ended.

He had always wanted to travel the Avalon Peninsula. He loved the beauty of the ocean and the country roads that wound their way in and out of the many inlets and coves.

Somehow he got to talking about his past. He fell in love after high school, had two children, but the relationship had recently broken up. Apparently, there was no marriage.

A time of healing was needed – maybe that's why he suddenly took off for Newfoundland. Those were his words. He wrote down his thoughts and feelings in his diary. He pulled the diary from his pack to show me. He said that maybe he would give it to his children one day.

The daily readings at Mass speak of Moses. Hidden from birth, set adrift on the waters, fleeing to a foreign land after murdering the Egyptian, called by God to set his people free, leading God's people through the wilderness, across the Red Sea, into the Promised Land. Moses was a man on the move.

Vatican II described the Church as a pilgrim people of God. Saint Ignatius of Loyola considered himself a pilgrim. Jesus calls us to follow him, to be pilgrims on the way.

I like the image of pilgrim. As pilgrims, we don't know the way ahead. Each day calls us into mystery, to faithfulness and trust. We place one foot in front of the other. Each day brings its own pain and its own beauty. We depend on the kindness of others. We pray on the providence of God.

That young man from Nova Scotia was on a pilgrimage. Maybe he wouldn't know to call it that. But I could sense that the journey was doing something to him. Maybe I'm just reading too much into it. Why, then, does the memory of that short hour's drive linger? I don't know exactly. I'm just grateful for having stopped for a hitchhiker on the side of an empty road.

When gratitude lingers in your heart, it speaks something of God. When that happens, stop – and listen.

God: A Three-letter Word

As I get older, I realize that I know less and less about God.

God – a simple three-letter word. I can pronounce the word "God" with the same energy and breath as I pronounce the words "cat," "dog" or "mouse." But, that's the heart of the problem. Given our ability to speak of "God" in the same way we speak of any other "thing," we fall into the trap of thinking of God as simply another "thing" or "person." God becomes a category just like any other category.

And not only do we see this God as simply one other being or thing, we have "supersized" God, emphasized God's "male-ness" and, for the most part, have placed God "outside" and "above" this world.

Given this perceived synonymy of God with all the other stuff of the world, we then feel a need to prove or disprove God's existence, using the same kind of reasoning as we would in proving or disproving the existence of cheese on the moon or the dynamics of climate change.

But such arguments and counter-arguments, while they may be stimulating for the mind, if not for the publisher's or writer's bank account, are generally useless when it comes to actually "proving" or "disproving" God.

As I mentioned at the beginning, I realize that I know less and less about God as the years advance. Furthermore, I seem more and more hesitant to use the word "God" – at least in any glib or assumed manner. Rather, I simply want to remove my shoes, bow my head and tread very softly.

When I speak of God, I am not speaking of simply another thing, like all the other things of the world. Rather, I am trying to speak of the ground of all things, the source of all things, the goal of all things. In a word, I am attempting to speak of Mystery – not as something to be solved, but as an experience to be entered into, with head bowed low.

The Christian tradition has long understood a need for "ground rules" when speaking of God. Three rules of God-language are generally accepted. The first is that when we speak of God, we are speaking of Mystery. The God of whom we speak is so apart and so different from the world – and so close and so intimate to the world – that God is Mystery, totally incomprehensible.

Despite this incomprehensibility of God, we need to use words to talk of God. God is Father, Transcendent, Immanent, Holy, Truth, Beauty, Good, Love, Merciful, Wisdom, Fire, Wind … God Is Who Is. But words are limited. And so, our second ground rule states that we always speak of God indirectly. No one image can ever encompass the fullness of God. We need many images of God. These images point towards God, but never fully comprehend or encompass God.

These first two rules imply a third: that images of God are just that, images, and cannot be taken literally. The literal is too narrow for the infinite, unbounded, everlasting God.

Two important implications spring from these three rules of God-talk.

First, our knowledge of God and our knowing God are two different things. The debates about the existence or non-existence of God are abundant *ad nauseam*. But to know God – that only seems to happen in the deepest, most silent recesses of our heart. We never grasp God. We simply enter into the ineffable mystery of God.

Second, the incomprehensibility of God invites us to a profound humility in our utterances. Who really knows the "mind of God"? Scripture plainly stresses the fact that God's ways are not our ways. And Job had to learn the hard way that he knew nothing of God.

The next time you use the word "God," be attentive. It may have only three letters, but never in the history of humanity did three simple letters mean so much.

The Catholic Imagination

The 2010 winner of the Templeton Prize (valued at $1.49 million US), the largest annual award given to an individual, was Professor Francisco Ayala of the University of California, Irvine. The prize is given to those who make an exceptional contribution to affirming life's spiritual dimension. Previous winners have included such religious luminaries as Mother Teresa, Billy Graham and Brother Roger, founder of the Taizé community. Less well-known recipients have included scientist-philosophers/theologians such as the Benedictine Stanley Jaki, the Anglican John Polkinghorne and Father Michael Heller of Poland, all of whom have made significant contributions to the faith-science dialogue.

Professor Ayala is no exception. As an evolutionary geneticist and molecular biologist, he contends that science and religion are not in conflict, but in fact have much to contribute to the flourishing of the other.

Over the years, I have dipped into Ayala's writings and ideas. His ideas always seemed to ring true; they resonated with me. Was he Catholic? I wondered. Sure enough, the Templeton Prize website describes Ayala as a former Dominican priest. Not Jesuit, but Dominican. But that's OK.

There's something about the Catholic imagination. It's hard to define, yet it has a certain texture. It sees the world in a certain way. It sticks out somehow. Maybe that is what I picked up in the writings and interviews of Professor Ayala – a sort of Catholic sensibility.

The divine and the human kiss in Jesus Christ. That fact has changed the world, changed how we view the world. Matter takes on meaning and depth. Faith and reason join hands in comprehension. Belief strengthens understanding – which in turn nourishes belief. Body and soul, heaven and earth, night and day cease their dualistic battles and grow attentive to each other.

Flannery O'Connor, the celebrated American Catholic novelist, once wrote of the Eucharist, "If it's just a symbol, then to hell with it." Our faith is incarnational, fleshy, meaty. We gnaw on the flesh and slurp the blood, as the more literal translation of "Eat my body and drink my blood" is wont to say.

The "dearest freshest, deep down things" of the Jesuit Victorian poet Gerard Manley Hopkins describes the same thing. There is a depth to creation, to life, to ourselves that we can never fully comprehend or imagine. That's the Catholic sensibility, the Catholic imagination, the Catholic sacramental.

So, when you enter the life of faith, don't leave your brains – or your sense of beauty and awe – at the door. Faith and reason, reason and emotion, certitude and questioning, all the ups and downs, the ins and outs of life get mixed together in the Catholic cauldron.

Our faith is what we say it is: truly catholic, truly universal.

Our Genetic Heritage: In the Image of God

I always figured that I harboured a beast within. The kind of beast that does the things I don't want to do and does not do the things I want to do. Saint Paul had the same problem (Romans 7:15). Now I know the reason why.

I can blame it all on the "caveman" within me. *Science* magazine has just reported the first partial genome of Neanderthals. According to the study, Neanderthals probably interbred with humans, and most of us carry up to 4 percent Neanderthal DNA. *Homo neanderthalensis* were coterminous with *Homo sapiens* thousands of years ago, but our Neanderthal cousins did not survive. Some of their DNA did.

Since the mid-1970s, we have known that the genomes (the entire genetic complement of an organism, comprising all its genes and DNA) of chimps and humans differ by only 2 percent.

This small difference is really much larger than it seems; a lot more than 2 percent of our proteins will differ by at least one amino acid from the genome sequence in chimps. Since proteins are essential for building and maintaining our bodies, a single difference can have substantial effects.

Regardless, all this recent evidence confirms the fact that we and our primate cousins share a common ancestor. Apparently, we split off from this common ancestor about six to seven million years ago. As the Virginia Slims cigarette ad of 1968 so proudly proclaimed, "You've come a long way, baby."

We have indeed come a long way. We are seven billion strong – and growing. We have essentially "humanized" the planet, with Bill McKibben's now classic *The End of Nature* (1989) signalling the end of the wild. According to the Jesuit paleontologist and mystic, Pierre Teilhard de Chardin (1881–1955), the universe has come to reflect back on itself in and through the human.

Contemporary science strengthens the fact that we are indeed of the earth. The words "human" and "humus" share the same etymological root. We are *adam,* from *adamah,* a Hebrew word meaning "ground." We are indeed human, of the earth.

At the same time, our faith tells us that we are made in the image and likeness of God. Rooted in the earth, we reach out to heaven. As "image of God," we are created as relational – related in love to God, to each other and to all creation. Genetics tells us that we are related to all other creatures on the biological level. Our faith tells us that we are related to all that ever was, ever is and ever will be, on the spiritual level. Our genes may be up to 4 percent Neanderthal. That is a cause for wonder. But our entire person, body and soul, is 100 percent in God. That fact should simply blow our mind.

OCTOBER

Thanksgiving

Climb the mountains and get their good tidings.
Nature's peace will flow into you as sunshine flows into trees.
The winds will blow their own freshness into you,
and the storms their energy,
while cares will drop off like autumn leaves.

—John Muir (1838–1914, Scottish-born American
conservationist, founder of the Sierra Club,
Father of the American National Parks
and patron saint of American environmentalism)

M aybe that is why I like hiking in the mountains north of Vancouver – it lets my cares drop like autumn leaves. Not long ago, a hiking buddy and I managed to ascend (and descend) the mountains in a ten-hour hike. It took us up an old logging road, in behind the Lions (+1600-metre twin peaks in the North Shore mountains north of Vancouver), where snow from last winter still lingered in the cold, drafty, north-facing slopes, along the meandering Howe Sound Crest Trail, around this and that mountain, and back down again to our starting point. I returned home somewhat sorer than when I started, but deeply grateful for the fullness of the day.

Thanksgiving Day was inaugurated by the Canadian Parliament in 1957 to give thanks to "Almighty God for the bountiful harvest with which Canada has been blessed." For many, the reference to God has quietly slipped away, but for all, the tradition continues to be important.

On my hike, I had much for which to give thanks. Thanks for my health and strength that permitted me to persist for ten hours on the trail. Thanks for a safe day. Thanks for the freedom and means to leave my home and travel to the mountains. Thanks for the beauty of mountain hemlock, amabilis fir, and yellow cypress, massive and statuesque. Thanks for the splash of red, yellow and orange of the oval-leafed blueberry, huckleberry, azalea and rhododendron. Thanks for the foggy wisps caressing the Lions with their cool embrace.

Eucharistia is Greek for "thanksgiving." Our daily Eucharist is an act of thanksgiving – thanksgiving for the saving mystery of Jesus Christ. Thanksgiving is thus at the heart of our faith.

However, it is not always easy to be thankful. We are often too side-tracked by our fears or our preoccupations to give much thought to the eucharistic soul of our lives. How often we lament the lack of this or that, oblivious to the abundance of so much. Simple inconveniences cloud our vision. We forget the generosity of others, the simple fact that none of us could live without the work, the intelligence and the ingenuity of countless people unknown to us. How often we take the necessities of life for granted – our food, our water, our warmth and protection, none of which would be possible without the basic and indispensable services offered by healthy ecosystems.

When you find it difficult to give thanks, pray for the grace to be thankful. Be patient with yourself. Gratitude will come. It is a gift. It frees us, it makes us humble and aware. It calls us into relationship and union.

I am indeed grateful for this day. I awaken, alive, breathing, heart pumping. Who knows what this day will bring – joy or sadness, hope or despair. But in and through it all, what I plead for is an open and gracious heart. Be thankful, if only for the smallest of things. Let gratitude become a habit. Before you know it, not a day will pass without a word of thanks.

A blessed Thanksgiving to you – on Thanksgiving Day and always.

Let Those with Eyes See

"They all look green to me."

Thus did my friend reply in her inimitable, sardonic manner to my animated naming of the passing trees as *black* spruce, *white* spruce, *white* pine, *red* pine and eastern *white* cedar. Despite my initial protests to her nugget of truth, I did see that she had a point. They did all look green.

I love walking through the forest after a good windstorm. Trees snapped off, blown over, uprooted. All part of the dynamic "ordered chaos" of a forest. Like every other living being, trees, if they live long enough – or rather, grow tall enough – will eventually be killed by something. For tall trees, wind can be the great destroyer.

What caught my sight during a recent post-windstorm walk were a series of snapped and cut red alder. Red alder (*Alnus rubra*), the most common deciduous tree in these parts, grows quickly on exposed mineral soil. That's why you see them so often along roads, old logging trails and river banks and flats.

This particular tree is described as "red" for good reason. Freshly cut or wounded wood or bark flashes forth with a vivid red-orange stain. The recent windstorm (and subsequent salvage cutting by park officials) had exposed such inner alder red in several places along my usual path. These freshly killed trees, their fatal red wounds gaping through the green-grey forest, were obvious to the pedestrian eye.

Chemists have obviously taken an interest in this reddish-orange colour. What to us is red is a series of natural diaryl-heptanoid glycosides that go by the names of (5S)-1,7-bis(3,4-dihydroxyphenyl)-5-O-(6-O-benzoyl-β-D-glucopyranosyl)-heptan-3-one and (5S)-1,7-bis(3,4-dihydroxyphenyl)-5-O-(6-O-vanilloyl-β-D-glucopyranosyl)-heptan-3-one. Just thought you'd want to know this. These three compounds are considered novel to red alder and have been the source of dyes and medicines for the indigenous peoples of the Pacific Northwest.

To my friend, all the trees were obviously – and rightly – green. For most of us, the red alder stain is simply that, a red stain.

But there's always more to life than meets the eye. For some, the human person is simply a naked ape, a vehicle of selfish genes, a complex firing of neurons, an accident in the great scheme of things. For Christians, the human is created in the image of God. The former description rests on the biological level. The latter description rests on the spiritual level. Both statements purport to describe truth.

However, the biological description is often presented as the *only* description of what it means to be human. The spiritual description should be able to include the biological level and carry it to deeper levels of intellectual and affective engagement.

The red alder is aptly named. So are all those other "green trees." But these simple green trees possess a depth and breadth that is not readily evident to the casual observer. Such depth requires a more discerning gaze, a contemplative spirit.

Maybe that is why Jesus constantly reminded his listeners to have eyes that see – and ears that hear – the deep, abiding glory of God.

Saint Kateri Tekakwitha:
She Who Feels Her Way Ahead

Catholic saints are a weird lot. Through no obvious power of their own, they do great things.

Across the years of time and the divides of culture and language, saints entice us, mystify us, intrigue us, maybe even irritate us. Strange stories and legends build up around them – stories of taming wolves, bodily incorruptibility, ecstatic union with the divine Spouse – and stories of downright unbelievable feats of love and generosity.

I attended a Mass of Thanksgiving for the canonization of Kateri Tekakwitha. Hundreds of people poured into the magnificent Oratory of Saint Joseph on the slopes of Montreal's Mount Royal to give thanks for this young Mohawk woman whom the Church declared a saint on October 21, 2012.

Kateri was born in 1656 to a Christian Algonquin woman and a Mohawk chief in what is now upstate New York (in the town of Auriesville). A smallpox outbreak took her parents and brother when she was just four; she survived, but was left with weak eyes and a pockmarked face. Eventually, she met some Jesuit missionaries. These Blackrobes impressed Kateri by their courteous manners and their piety. On Easter Sunday 1676, at twenty years of age, she was baptized. Persecution by her family eventually forced her to move to the Jesuit mission at Kahnawake, across from Montreal, where she died at the young age of twenty-four.

Saint Kateri is North America's first Aboriginal saint. Impressive as that is, the Church goes even further and states that Saint Kateri is now a model for the universal Church. She goes beyond the regional, the national, the continental and the ethnic or cultural, bridging all peoples for all times.

It seems that canonizations in the Church do not often happen without a context. As the Truth and Reconciliation Commission crosses Canada to engage the legacy of the Indian Residential Schools, Saint Kateri emerges on the scene. I wonder what healing we will witness in her name.

Saints unsettle us. They bridge our well-guarded chasms, our misunderstandings and our ruptures. Their very existence questions our deeply held fears and blindness. Maybe that's the greatest miracle.

In some small way, I witnessed that miracle at the Mass of Thanksgiving celebrated in French, English and Mohawk on the slopes of Mount Royal. I thought to myself, Who would have predicted several hundred years ago that a young, sickly Mohawk woman would one day gather together in prayer long-standing traditional enemies? She bridged the Aboriginal and European cultures, the Mohawk and Algonquin cultures, the world of belief and unbelief, the world of linguistic and cultural tensions.

Because of Kateri's weakened eyes, as a result of smallpox, she was extremely sensitive to the brightness of daylight. She was thus given the name Tekakwitha – she who feels her way ahead. What a most apt description of the life of faith.

After the celebration, I descended the slopes of Mount Royal filled with a deep sense of hope. As I and the many others walking down the mountain filed past each other, each intent on his or her own world, busy with this or that, I thought that, if only for a moment, we were one. We had left behind our differences in the name of the Lily of the Mohawks. That is miracle enough for me. Saint Kateri, pray for us.

Beautiful Hands of the Nail-biter Priest

I wish I had beautiful hands. I sometimes find myself gazing at other people's fingers. Ever so discreetly, my eyes wander along the length of their fingers. I am struck by the fineness of form, the strong, well-manicured nails. I marvel at nails not bitten and cuticles not infected by hangnails.

A friend of mine, now long deceased, once proclaimed that I don't have the hands of a priest. "What do the hands of a priest look like?" I protested. I had just gotten back from several weeks in the field, and the fieldwork had inflicted its normal battery of bruises, scrapes and cuts.

Most of my hand wounds are self-inflicted. I'm a nail biter. I can't remember when I first fell into the habit – maybe in the womb. But, one day back in the mist of time, I began to bite my nails.

Call it a sign of neurotic things hidden, unfulfilled desires, subconscious anxiety, oral fixation or downright bad habit, but I have been picking at my nails for decades. Freud would probably have had a field day.

Periods of calm sometimes prevail, permitting the nails to actually grow. But eventually, they are cut back to their usual painful stumps.

An anonymous poet has written a poem entitled "The Beautiful Hands of a Priest." A few lines will give you a feel for the poem.

> When the hour of death comes upon us
> may our courage and strength be increased
> By seeing raised over us in anointing
> the beautiful hands of a priest.

For some, the poem may be too sweet and sugary, sappy with pious drivel. For others, it speaks a truth that only such words can muster. For me, it's a call to realize that no matter what the state of my hands is, they possess their own sacred power.

The power to forgive, to caress, to consecrate, to bless, to hold, to invite, to support … to love.

There are times when I am embarrassed by the state of my hands. Why can't my fingers look like those of most people? Is my heart so disfigured that my hands show it?

But I am reminded of the words of Saint Paul: "I do not understand my own actions. For I do not do what I want, but I do the very thing I hate" (Romans 7:15). That describes well how I experience my nail biting. We do indeed see things through a glass darkly. God does indeed choose the weak. That he makes the weak strong is our only hope.

So the next time I lift my hands in blessing or in consecration, I will try to accept the fact that my hands may not be that beautiful. They may be marked by my anxiety, or whatever. But that is all I have to offer my God. In the words of the *Suscipe* of Saint Ignatius Loyola, "Take, Lord, and receive all my liberty, my memory, my understanding, my entire will, all I have and call my own. You have given all to me."

To you, Lord, I return it – hangnails and all.

Gorillas, Malaria and the Spiritual Dignity of the Human Person

The Bible and the Catholic theological tradition claim that we are made in the image and likeness of God. We are made for God, for union with God in faith, hope and love. We are hearers of the Word, called to welcome the Spirit of God already present in our hearts.

It seems that we are also made to receive much more. A recent study has confirmed that humans got the deadliest form of malaria from our western gorilla cousins. As humans, we are infected by five *Plasmodium* species, with *Plasmodium falciparum* causing by far the greatest morbidity and mortality in humans. Each year, there are several hundred million cases of clinical malaria and more than one million deaths from malaria (over 2,700 deaths per day). It used to be thought that the bad air (*mal aire*) of swamps caused such deaths. We now know, of course, that mosquitoes, regular inhabitants of swamps, act as the vector for the blood-borne malarial disease.

We receive a lot of other infectious diseases from our feathered and non-feathered friends. Chimpanzees are the source of HIV-1, the major cause of AIDS. Think of the public health issues surrounding swine flu and avian or bird flu. Mad cow disease, West Nile virus, SARS and rabies are but a few examples of the many other so-called zoonotic viruses that have jumped from animals into humans, causing serious outbreaks from time to time. In fact, of the more than 1,400 human pathogens, over 60 percent are zoonotics. Some animals may be our best friends, but there can be a price to pay for such close contact over the millennia.

Seen from this perspective, nature seems to pursue its own course without any regard for the spiritual dignity of humans. Yet we also know that behind humankind and nature there exists a unity. We call that unity God.

I don't claim to comprehend this unity of tensions. Many are tempted to choose one pole or the other. For some, materialism defines everything. For others, spiritualism is a constant temptation. For materialists, the earth is all there is. For spiritualists, why worry about earth when it's heaven we seek? But, as humans, we're both – body and soul, spirit and nature, heaven and earth. Humans are not "either/or," but "both/and."

Monisms oversimplify the human person. Rather, we're like those mighty trees – rooted in the earth and reaching out to heaven – made in the image of God and products of the stardust of the universe.

Spanish Jesuits of the early 1600s are credited with introducing the bark of the *Chichona* tree from Peru into Europe. Quinine, an extract from what is sometimes known as Jesuit's bark, was an early successful remedy for malaria. Those early Jesuits would have known little of the cause and spread of malaria, but I suspect that their efforts to develop a possible cure for malaria revealed their denial of any final opposition between spirit and flesh. They would not have known of the gorilla–malaria connection, but they would have rejoiced in the fact that the origin and goal of nature and humankind are one and the same.

NOVEMBER

Do Monkeys Go to Heaven?

W hen it comes to the Christian notion of the "end times," we can often think in this way. Why worry about the Earth when we're all trying to get into heaven? Why worry about nature when it is the salvation of the person that we seek? Or, more explicitly, why worry about the salvation of the body when it is the soul that is all-important?

In the end, so it goes, Earth, nature and body are not what counts. What really counts in the end, some believe, are heaven and humans, or, more importantly, heaven and the human soul. This assumption, while commonly accepted by many Christians, is, in fact, heretical.

This assumption is heretical because it fails to consider the fact that Christianity is committed to matter. Think of the Word made flesh, the incarnation, the Holy Spirit active and at home in all creation, the resurrection of the body of Jesus Christ, the final fulfillment of all creation in the Trinity, when God will be "all in all" (1 Corinthians 15:28).

For a long time we have focused on the destiny of the individual person as we grappled with notions of heaven, hell, purgatory and limbo. Graphic accounts of the hereafter, particularly of the fires and fumes of hell, marked many a Lenten mission. Little attention was afforded the notion of a collective destiny of all creation.

As Christians, we are a people of the "future" – in the sense of promise and hope. The Kingdom of God, the Promised Land, the resurrection of Jesus Christ, the Second Coming of Christ – all these point towards a future that is expressed fully only in God.

We know that we are incomplete and unfinished. Tears are still shed, our hearts long for peace and justice in the world. Hope is a theological virtue, rooted in the promise of the resurrection of Christ.

For in the resurrection of Christ, the universe radically changed. It would never be the same again. The promise of God broke through the chains of death and violence to reveal life and light at the heart of creation.

In the resurrection, the material body of Jesus Christ was taken into God. The resurrection signalled the life-giving promise of God. The beginning of the divinization of the world had taken hold. Jesus became the firstborn of all creation, the beginning of the transformation of the entire universe.

All creation groans and longs for final fulfillment. Creation "waits with eager longing for the revealing of the children of God," groaning in hope for "the freedom of the glory of the children of God" (Romans 8:18-23).

So, do monkeys go to heaven? If we believe in the resurrection of Jesus Christ and the final fulfillment of all creation in the Love of God, then yes, monkeys do go to heaven.

We hope that all creation will reach fulfillment in God, but such fulfillment will no doubt depend on the "level of being" of each creature. God relates to each creature on its own terms. This is mysterious. However, our faith speaks of a fecund, loving God who embraces all creation in the vivifying Spirit, and in Christ, in whom all things hold together – all things, monkeys and humans alike.

Stumbling and Fumbling in the Dark

I hike up Grouse Mountain (North Vancouver, BC) at least once a week. Not by the so-called Grouse Grind, but rather by a trail just to the east of the Grind called the BC Mountaineering Club trail. It's a bit longer than the Grind, composed of many more switchbacks and, in my opinion, is a much more pleasant trail.

My companions and I normally hit the trailhead at 7 a.m. In the late fall, that means donning headlamps for at least the first thirty minutes of the climb. We must look a funny lot, not long out of bed, stumbling and fumbling our way among roots and rocks, headlamps lancing the dark – and rain trickling down our necks.

Last week, we got to musing about life – as one is often wont to do while out on the trail. Being in the woods has a way of calling us back to basics. We thought, Isn't life often like stumbling along an early morning uphill trail in the darkened world, amidst dripping rain? Not always, to be sure, but Saint Paul himself admitted that we often see through a glass darkly (1 Corinthians 13:12).

Our personal and family lives can often look like stumbling and fumbling in the dark. We don't know exactly where we're going, or if we do, how to get there. How we ended up as we did is often just as mysterious. Our global lives can take on that same sense of waywardness.

We seem to hear very little about nuclear weapons these days. At least, that is my sense. Climate change, with its predicted and documented nefarious consequences for both human and non-human life, has captured our imagination. In the meantime, silent, still and even more menacing, I think, is our fascination with "mutual assured destruction" – the ultimate pro-life issue, it seems.

The nuclear club boasts thousands of active and operational warheads. According to the Arms Control Association website, in 2013 China had 240 warheads, France less than 300, the United Kingdom 225, with the Russian and American heavyweights boasting a combined total of 9,615 nuclear warheads. Fledgling India possesses up to 100 warheads, Israel has between seventy-five and 200, and Pakistan between ninety and 100 warheads. To top it all off, Iran, North Korea and Syria are vying to join the nuclear team.

For the life of me, I cannot tell you the difference between having 1,000 and 5,000 operational nuclear warheads. This is where a few seems a little too many. Planes are in the air, submarines ply the deeps, and men and women are being trained to "press the button." Nations are in nuclear-ready mode, with weapons of mass destruction standing by for the executive order. We're afraid of something. We're willing to risk a lot before that fear. Sounds like a lot of fumbling and stumbling in the dark.

Near the top of Grouse we were welcomed by the lighting of the dawn from on high. Our gait quickened as we approached the summit. The freshly fallen snow added glimmer to the early morning brightness. In several weeks, Advent will beckon us into the light of Christ. We need this season of light amidst the growing darkness of winter. May the light of Christ guide us through our stumbling and fumbling in the dark – both personal and nuclear.

Death of a Jesuit

They trudged through the fresh snow, whitened and whipped by the biting winter winds. They had come, young and old, to accompany their beloved pastor to his final resting place. The grave had been prepared. A mound of partly frozen earth, covered by artificial green turf, broke the silent white expanse of the cemetery. The black hearse waited patiently.

Along with hundreds of other mourners, I had attended the funeral of Rev. William Addley, SJ, that morning. A long-time pastor at the Jesuit parish of Our Lady of Lourdes in Toronto, Father Bill was well loved by many. Thousands had attended the days of wake held in the church. Long lines of people waited to kneel and pray one final time beside their faithful guide and shepherd.

Catholic wakes are generally a time of great unity. People come to pay their respects to the family. People the family hasn't seen in years, maybe. Hugs, laughter, conversation, memories, silent sitting in solidarity. Wakes bring out the best in us.

I would love to know who crafted the funeral liturgy. If celebrated well, it is pure genius. For some reason, it helps us grieve and cry well. The Word of God, the song of the angels, holy water, sweet-smelling incense, candles, wine, bread, white vestments, and movement with meaning.

As with all good liturgy, funerals invite us into sacred time and space. The meaning of death is addressed with realism and hope. Death has been conquered, so we are invited to enter into its darkness, only to be led into further light.

Rest assured that the pain of loss and separation is by no means denied. The funeral liturgy admits the sharp, poisoned sting of death. That is why death can never be engaged simply with words or the reasoning of the mind. Death is irrational, un-reasonable, not welcomed. Because of that, death can be engaged only in ritual, in that suspension of normal time and space. Death can be engaged only in and through the loving mystery of God.

After the funeral, about 200 faithful travelled several hours by bus and car to the Jesuit cemetery in the city of Guelph, south-west of Toronto. The small cemetery is surrounded by 600 acres of beautiful farmland, wetland and forest, a property stewarded by the Jesuits and their co-workers for decades. Father Bill began his Jesuit life on that property when he entered the Jesuit noviti- ate on August 14, 1964. Forty-eight years later, he had returned to rest on that land forever.

A winter squall had gained energy as the people gathered around the opened earth. Song sheets flapped in numbed hands. Voices sang their song of lament. The priest's words of consola- tion filtered through the cold winter air.

Before Bill's body was lowered into the ground, everyone gathered up handfuls of clay-rich earth, held it, and let it fall on Bill's casket. From the earth we came, into the bowels of the earth we return.

The day of the funeral was my birthday. A strange way to celebrate a birthday, you may think. But, amidst our tears, we celebrated the goodness and kindness of Bill. As Jesuit Provin- cial, Father Bill had accepted me into the Society of Jesus. He had been so kind to me – and to countless others over the years.

I can think of no better way to celebrate life than at a funeral.

Tsunamis and a Benevolent God

At 5:02 p.m. on Monday, November 18, 1929, an under- water earthquake occurred in the North Atlantic, registering 7.2 on the Richter scale. Two hundred and sixty-five kilometres to the north, the people of the fishing communities that dotted the south coast of Newfoundland felt the ground tremors. They could never imagine what was to happen.

Two hours later, it struck. Tsunami waves hit the coast at 40 kilometres per hour, raising sea levels up to 27 metres. The people never had a chance. Over a period of thirty minutes, three successive waves slammed into the unsuspecting coast, destroying all in its path, washing twenty-eight people to their deaths – and causing extensive damage to coastal communities.

The Newfoundland tsunami of 1929 obviously pales in comparison to the 2004 Indian Ocean tsunami that killed over 230,000 people in fourteen countries. And the death toll for the 2011 Japanese tsunami was nearly 21,000 people. However, the Newfoundland story shows that even in areas not known for earthquake activity, tsunamis can indeed happen.

How may we understand a benevolent God in the context of natural disasters such as earthquakes, floods and volcanoes? Many answers are given, from punishment for sin to the notion that the great flood of Genesis altered the earth in ways that promote the natural disasters of today. Insurance companies simply call them "acts of God" and leave it at that. Such explanations are not helpful.

The writer of Genesis proclaimed creation to be good. And that includes the tectonic structure of planet Earth, which consists of several major plates and many minor ones. These tectonic plates are mobile, riding over the asthenosphere, the highly viscous portion of the upper mantle. These plates move in relation to one another, and the relative movement causes earthquakes and volcanoes, builds mountains and deepens ocean trenches.

The earth has a history, a story. And that story continues to unfold in ways that are slow – and in ways that are ferocious and fiery. The Himalayas rise at a rate of 5 millimetres per year as the Indo-Australian plate pushes its way into the Eurasian plate. The region is seismically active; thousands have died in earthquakes over the past century.

Japan – and coastal British Columbia – are also located in a seismically active part of the world, the so-called Ring of Fire. Stretching in a horseshoe shape from southern Chile north to

Alaska, across to Kamchatka, down through Japan and ending up in New Zealand far to the south, the Ring of Fire accounts for 90 percent of the world's earthquakes.

This is the Earth that we call home. It's an active, energetic, ever-changing Earth. The Earth's future is unfolding. It is not fixed.

As to why a good God would permit natural disaster, I have no answer – because it is the wrong question. A volcano does what a volcano does. An earthquake does what an earthquake does.

Any other way and the world would simply be a puppet on a divine string.

Saint Peter's Basilica and Occupy Vancouver

Before you enter Saint Peter's Basilica, you must pass through Saint Peter's Square (Piazza San Pietro). It's a magnificent elliptical space (240 metres wide) constructed during the pontificates of Alexander VII (1655–1667) and Clement IX (1667–1669). Colonnades embrace the square and all who enter.

The square may be thought of as "liminal" or "in-between" space, where boundaries are dissolved and people may enter freely on the way to somewhere.

In Christian terms, we may think of liminal space as connecting heaven and earth or body and soul. It's that place where we venture out of our old ways into new, as yet untrod, future ways. Saint Paul would have understood it as that space between the way of the flesh and the way of the spirit, that in-between place and time when we wrestle with our soul on the way to healing, conversion and spiritual freedom.

Occupy Vancouver was located in just such a liminal space in front of the Vancouver Art Gallery, part of Robson Square.

Robson Square may not be Saint Peter's Square, but they both provide that free space for people to gather – and even to protest.

The Occupy Vancouver website explained the movement in these terms:

Occupy Vancouver – A Non Violent Movement for Social, Economic and Political Change

We, the Ninety-Nine Percent, come together with our diverse experiences to transform the unequal, unfair, and growing disparity in the distribution of power and wealth in our city and around the globe. We challenge corporate greed, corruption, and the collusion between corporate power and government. We oppose systemic inequality, militarization, environmental destruction, and the erosion of civil liberties and human rights. We seek economic security, genuine equality, and the protection of the environment for all.

The increasing global inequalities in power and wealth have been the concern of Catholic social teaching for decades, particularly during the pontificates of John Paul II (1978–2005) and Benedict XVI (2005–2013).

One may argue about the efficacy and legitimacy of the "occupy movements" proliferating around the world. No social movement, or human institution, for that matter, comes fault-free.

Regardless of where you stand on the matter, one thing is certain. Occupy Vancouver and the Vatican are speaking the same language. The messengers may be different. The form of delivery may be different. But the heart of the message is the same.

The open space in front of the Vancouver Art Gallery and the open space in front of Saint Peter's Basilica embrace the same desires of the human heart.

DECEMBER

Advent and U2

My favourite rock band is the Irish group U2. And one of my favourite songs is U2's "I Still Haven't Found What I'm Looking For." It's the second track from U2's 1987 album *The Joshua Tree*. (You can listen to it on YouTube if you want to jog your memory.)

This song reminds me so much of Advent, which is often described as a period of waiting. It's that time of the year when the beginnings of winter slow us down a little. The snows soften our cities and lives, hushing our surroundings. Advent slows us down as the snowy paths slow our faltering steps.

I simply love Advent. It's often a very busy time of year – the end of the semester, the beginning of exams, the push of deadlines. At the same time, our Advent liturgies invite us to wait and long for something – or Someone – who matters far beyond our daily labours.

We pause, we listen, we long for the coming of Christ – for the birth of our Messiah, for the birth of the Trinity in our naked now, for the Second Coming of Love, when all our tears will be wiped away.

I am well aware that I still haven't found what I'm looking for. I may have my Jesuit vocation, my academic degrees, even my Starbucks card and my Visa card, but, to be honest, I know that I long for something much more. Maybe that is why I love Advent. The beginning of the new liturgical year, the beginning of the winter season, mimics the longings of my heart, laden with its dust bunnies and plaque.

As U2 proclaim, I know that my Saviour has broken the bonds of my imprisonment and loosed the chains of my doubt, but I know that my heart and soul never cease to long for something. According to Ron Rolheiser, OMI, this longing is holy, but often my restlessness seems downright unruly. And so I need Advent. It's my annual dose of spiritual sanity, my annual spiritual check-up, so to speak, that calls me to continue my pilgrimage of waiting and longing. Waiting not to find what I'm looking for, but rather to be found by the One who longs to be born within me.

Advent with Winnie-the-Pooh

I found myself dancing at a Rexall drugstore today. It was somewhere between the condoms and the painkillers, I think. The strangest of places, I must admit, but there you go, the grace of God knows no bounds.

In Toronto, at the corner of College and Bay, gliding through the aisles of the drugstore with a lift to my feet and a lilt to my heart. And the source of such public behaviour? Over the store's PA system emanated the seductive voices of the Spinners, that long-running American soul group, with their 1975 hit song "They Just Can't Stop It (Games People Play)."

Whenever I hear that song, my body has to move.

Immediately to mind came another song that moves my heart. It's the one by Kenny Loggins, "House at Pooh Corner," based on the popular children's book of the same name.

It was the summer of 1982. I was terribly in love with Maureen, finishing my Master's of Science at the University of Florida, thinking about the Jesuit priesthood, and about to move from Florida back to Newfoundland. Needless to say, I was very confused. And this song was Maureen's and my song.

Maybe the journey of Christopher Robin and Winnie-the-Pooh was my journey "under the branches lit up by the moon." And I had indeed "wandered much farther … than I should" and I couldn't "seem to find my way back to the wood."

I eventually entered the Jesuits – and the rest is history. Maureen eventually married and had one son. In her late twenties, Maureen died of cancer.

As I write, I listen again to the journey of Christopher Robin and Pooh. Those summer days of 1982 have returned – at least for a moment. I dream of what life those days gave me. I muse on what could have been.

I don't know what causes me to dance when I hear the Spinners. But when I hear the song of Christopher Robin and Pooh, I know what it does to me – it gives me sadness, delight, lament, joy, and so much more. I wish I could explain it all, but I can't. It's downright impossible.

Maybe that's the way it should be. Life is simply life – but it can be complex. We go on in time, each moment and each person affecting us eternally. We're often oblivious to it all, caught up as we are with the quotidian of life. But I hazard to say that love and pain are never too far below the surface. Nor should they be, I suppose. That's what makes life so good, so pure. We are crafted into the image of God. Never hard-wired, but rather moulded into love by Love.

Be attentive, therefore. Advent is a time of waiting, of keeping alert. The next time you are moved by something, no matter what it may be, rest with it. Savour it, taste it, smell it and drink it in full … in a word, contemplate it. Let it take you where it will. Let it be an angel announcing to you the impossible, the forgotten, the misplaced.

For, in the end, all is grace – even as we make our way among the condoms and painkillers.

Grace of Winter Solstice

I didn't want to do it. They wouldn't miss me, surely, I thought. I had had a bit of a rough day, was feeling rather sorry for myself, and maybe even somewhat resentful. All I wanted to do was stay home and relax with a glass of red wine. Or maybe I simply wanted to stay away and hide.

Either way, it was not to be.

I pulled myself out of my pit, got dressed, left the house and headed out on the road. I listened to the CBC news along the way. Thankfully, it distracted me.

After parking, I headed down the blackened neighbour-hood streets. The evening chill under the cloudless night sky refreshed me. I could even make out some constellations in the darkened heavens.

I entered the foyer, greeted a few people and proceeded on my way. People were gathering, shuffling, finding their place.

The first penitent arrived before me, then the second, the third, on into the depth of the night.

Who was I but the conduit, the lightning rod, in that strange, privileged place between heaven and earth. One stranger before another. Words of commission, words of omission. Words of regret, words of bewilderment. Words of consolation. Words of forgiveness.

With each person, with each profession, my heart trans-formed. It ached, it delighted, it wondered, it stood in awe before all who came my way. No script here, no words rehearsed. Just the raw stuff of life. Just the raw stuff of grace.

All this happened on the day of winter solstice – that time of the year that marks the beginning of winter and the shortest day of the year. People celebrate this return of the sun to the northern hemisphere by various celebrations meant to tap into the ancient rhythms of life and earth.

Unbeknownst to me, I had elected to mark the winter solstice in a Vancouver church celebrating the Sacrament of Reconciliation. I cannot think of a more appropriate thing to do on the shortest day of the year.

Reconciliation calls us back from the winter of our lives into the spring of rebirth. What better way to celebrate the turning of the northern hemisphere to the sun?

At Christmas, we bring the evergreen tree into our homes – that enduring reminder of the eternal youthfulness of life. Christmas – that time of the year when our sacred writings, the Scriptures, speak of erotic lovers, pregnancy, expectant waiting and longing. We hear stories of a virgin woman and a barren woman who both rejoice in the gift of pregnancy. We stand in awe before the truth of divinity enfleshed.

After celebrating the sacrament with countless people, I returned home graced. It was not my doing. Not at all. I am unable to squeeze grace from a stone. But from God, it oozes forth in abundance.

Christmas. That strange time of year when divinity is enfleshed, when all is grace. How I need that. How I need to celebrate the return of the Sun of God, the Son of God, into the cold, wintry crevices of my life.

Christmas Evergreen and Light

I helped a friend of mine cut a Christmas tree the other day. It was a balsam fir, a lovely, fragrant, symmetrical tree. Native to North America, balsam fir ranges from Newfoundland to Alberta in Canada.

When I was young, I loved going off into the woods to cut balsam fir Christmas trees with several of my buddies. We would make a day of it. Set a fire, cook beans and bacon, eat homemade bread, and brew some coffee or tea – sweetened, of course, with Carnation condensed milk.

Christmas is a time when we bring the evergreen of the forest into the warmth of our homes. At a time when the days shorten and the nights lengthen, when all the leaves have fallen and much of nature readies for the sleep of winter, we decorate our doors with sprigs of green branches and fill a welcome corner of our homes with the evergreen tree.

Just before Christmas, we also pass through the winter solstice – the shortest day of the year. The winter solstice occurs between December 20 and 23. In 2013 in Vancouver, we celebrated the winter solstice on December 21. The day length was 8 hours, 11 minutes and 59 seconds: the shortest day of the year. The next day we enjoyed a longer day of 8 hours, 12 minutes and 3 seconds – an increase of 4 seconds. We take heart as the days start getting longer.

It is not without reason that Christianity decided to place Christmas at this time of the year. As the people of the northern hemisphere celebrate the return of the sun to the boreal skies, Christianity celebrates the birth of "the light of the world." And into our homes is brought the tree that remains green throughout the death of winter. Christianity celebrates the Life that has come into the world to heal us, to save us, and to lead us to true life, even everlasting life.

Life and Light – that's what we celebrate at Christmas. The cosmic signs and natural rhythms lift their voices in honour and praise of the Life and Light of the World.

At the heart of our faith seems to be this relentless thrust towards life – human life, ecological life, planetary life, spiritual life, eternal life. Jesus said that he has come so we may have life – and life to the full (John 10:10). The spiritual life does not focus on spiritual things, but on *all* things and ways that promote life in its fullness.

Salvation is cosmic. All is included. Nothing is left out.

We celebrate Christmas in the dead of winter with the evergreen tree firmly rooted in our homes and the evergreen wreath of welcome on our doors. Christmas witnesses to our belief that even in the midst of the darkness, death and cold of winter lies the secret hint of light, life and warmth.

Passing on the Faith at Christmas

It is often thought that Christian faith is first and foremost a thing of the mind. Understand, then you will come to believe. Nothing could be further from the truth. Saint Anselm (1033–1109), a great intellect of the Middle Ages, put a different spin on things when he admitted that he does not seek to understand so that he may believe, but he believes in order to understand. Saint Augustine (354–430) professed as much when he stated that "I do not seek to understand that I may believe, but I believe in order to understand."

I am not denying the essential role of human reason in the life of faith. Faith and reason go together. Anselm said the same in his classic definition of theology as "faith seeking understanding." But faith is not primarily a product or function of reason.

Let's apply this to the season of Christmas. At Christmas, we celebrate the profound mystery of the incarnation of God – God becoming enfleshed in the person of Jesus Christ, born of the Virgin Mary.

However, most of us don't begin the season of Christmas grappling with the mystery and intricacies of "incarnation." We come at it in more oblique, more human ways – Christmas concerts and pageants, carolling, gift giving, food, drink and friendship, liturgy, poinsettias, decoration, Christmas trees, candles, colour, nativity scenes, walking to midnight Mass on a cold, snowy night, visiting family and friends, sending Christmas cards, preparing Christmas dinner, baking, visiting the sick and imprisoned, caring for those in need, and the list goes on.

And through it all, the mystery of "incarnation" seeps in, slowly, imperceptibly. Faith is not something taught. Rather, it is absorbed by the fabric of life such that it fills, quietly and mysteriously, every strand of our lives. We "learn" faith through osmosis. At a certain point, our minds yearn for a different form of learning. That's when we begin to "theologize" as we try to make sense of our prior human experience, both individual and collective.

So, this Christmas, don't worry too much about plumbing the depths of the mystery of the incarnation or questioning why God chose to become human. Celebrate Christmas to the full, enjoy each other, share your lives with others. In the process, you will live the incarnation – and in that way you will come to know.